AF766399

Information Dynamics in Virtual Worlds

CHANDOS
INFORMATION PROFESSIONAL SERIES

Series Editor: Ruth Rikowski
(email: Rikowskigr@aol.com)

Chandos' new series of books is aimed at the busy information professional. They have been specially commissioned to provide the reader with an authoritative view of current thinking. They are designed to provide easy-to-read and (most importantly) practical coverage of topics that are of interest to librarians and other information professionals. If you would like a full listing of current and forthcoming titles, please visit our web site www.chandospublishing.com or email info@chandospublishing.com or telephone +44 (0) 1223 499140.

New authors: we are always pleased to receive ideas for new titles; if you would like to write a book for Chandos, please contact Dr Glyn Jones on e-mail gjones@chandospublishing.com or telephone number +44 (0) 1993 848726.

Bulk orders: some organisations buy a number of copies of our books. If you are interested in doing this, we would be pleased to discuss a discount. Please contact on e-mail info@chandospublishing.com or telephone +44 (0) 1223 499140.

Information Dynamics in Virtual Worlds

Gaming and beyond

WOODY EVANS

CP
CHANDOS
PUBLISHING

Oxford Cambridge New Delhi

Chandos Publishing
Hexagon House
Avenue 4
Station lane
Witney
Oxford OX28 4BN
UK
Tel: +44 (0) 1993 848726
Email: info@chandospublishing.com
www.chandospublishing.com

Chandos Publishing is an imprint of Woodhead Publishing Limited

Woodhead Publishing Limited
80 High Street
Sawston
Cambridge CB22 3HJ
UK
Tel: +44 (0) 1223 499140 ext. 130
www.woodheadpublishing.com

First published 2011

ISBN: 978 1 84334 641 8

A catalogue record for this book is available from the British Library.

Typeset by RefineCatch Ltd, Bungay, Suffolk
Printed in the UK and USA.

This one is for Steven, who turned me on to *Dungeons & Dragons* just when I needed it the most.

Contents

Acknowledgements

Thanks to the library staff at Tarrant County College. We do good work together.

Thanks to my friends and family, especially to my wife Aubree.

Thanks to Glyn Jones, Barbara Quint, Paula Hane, R.U. Sirius, and all the editors and readers who have helped me to sharpen up.

If I'm better, I'm better because of all of you.

About the Author

Woody Evans is a public services librarian at Tarrant County College in Arlington, Texas. As a librarian and private researcher, he has worked for military, corporate, and academic organizations. His work can be read in *American Libraries, Library Journal, Searcher Magazine, ONLINE, Information Today, The Journal of Evolution and Technology, H+ Magazine, Mississippi Libraries, Rain Taxi Review of Books*, and others. His previous book from Chandos, *Building Library 3.0: Creating a Culture of Participation*, continues to receive wide praise in America and France. Contact him through woodyevans.wordpress.com.

Introduction

Virtual worlds, virtual reality, augmented reality, cyberspace – every few years the idea of alternative computer-generated worlds becomes popular for a while, then fades away again in the light of collective disdain. There is wild oscillation from glee to sneer. This has been happening for a while now. Whether the buzz is hologram games or virtual commerce, interest builds precipitously before 'the virtual' is again relegated to last year's fad.

Second Life was the flagship of the most recent run on virtual world cool, but five years after the big *Business Week* cover story (big buzz back in May, 2006: 'My Virtual Life'), *Second Life* and many other attempts at modelling alternative realities are looking very dated. None yet seem to be gentrifying.

More information is now generated than ever before in human history, and this wild growth is happening in ways that can only be approached through models, through virtual worlds. These virtual worlds are, in turn, generating more and more information about themselves; or, if you'd rather, the actors in these worlds are generating the information about themselves and their worlds – but these actors are not always human. Useage statistics, trade values for 'gold' and 'real estate', chat logs, and many other types of automated data grow daily for virtual worlds. Algorithms tattle on almost all and any inworld happenings. But, of course, such data is growing in our Real Life too, and that data from Real Life activities is best visualized with (again) virtual models.

In this wash of information, the Real and the virtual blend. The first halting spawn of this seemingly inevitable arrangement appear variously as location-aware phone apps, computer interfaces that rely on physical gesture, and the slow encroachment by social networking sites upon our actual face-to-face social lives (ever have a conversation in a pub about a conversation going on in Facebook?).

Those attentive to media, technology, and information concerns would do well to use this moment – this temporary lull in excitement for 'the virtual' at the beginning of the 2010s – to look at virtual worlds as they are *now*, and to look at the use and movement of information in virtual worlds, before these worlds (as we now know them) are gone.

This is because the virtual will become finally and terribly married to the Real.

It may seem strange to quote Wallace Stegner (1969) in this context, but in his famous 'Wilderness Letter' he lamented losing the chance 'to see ourselves single, separate, vertical and individual in the world, part of the environment of trees and rocks and soil, brother to the animals, part of the natural world and competent to belong in it'. For the moment, virtual worlds remain somewhat isolated, singular in their identities, and (as much as it can be said about an environment cooked up with coal-fired electricity on silicon, lithium, and acrylonitrile butadiene styrene) still in their natural state.

These worlds and their inhabitants are 'vertical' in their own contexts, 'individual' in their own ontologies.

Soon the Real World will be slick with traces of the virtual. In 2011 it is woefully obvious to say so, but more aspects of our lives are becoming mediated all the time; there may soon come a day when the notion of 'virtual worlds' is meaningless, because there will be no firm border between the virtual and the Real.

So here we look at information dynamics in virtual worlds. We do this to gather thoughts about information dynamics in virtual worlds generally, and also to prepare for a future understanding of the relationships between what's real, what's mediated, and what's human when all the boundaries start to slide.

Woody Evans
North Texas
Autumn 2010

Part I
Virtual Ontologies

1

Mapping virtual worlds

Abstract: Virtual worlds are many and varied. In investigating the scope of virtual communities, it is important to understand social and theoretical issues that impact online participants. Such issues as gender, ontology, socio-technological integration, and corporeal interface all impact exploration of virtual worlds.

Key words: theory, hyperreality, globalization, gender, actor-network theory, transhumanism.

Theory v. reality

So: what is a virtual world? We can tackle the question from many different directions. There are the metaphysical concerns about whether an experience in a virtual world is any less real than an experience in the conventional/consensual world of Real Life. How real is the virtual or our experience of the virtual? There's the epistemological route that considers whether a fully immersive virtual world is knowable in the same way as Real Life. How can we know that our experiences in it are any less real than 'reality'? We can look at virtual worlds from aesthetic perspectives, and we can judge our experiences in them in terms of ethics. Since this book is concerned with information, we'll only look at theory in a hard-nosed and practical way. Epistemological posturing doesn't mean squat if it can't help us to get the information to the people; what does it matter that we know X about world Y, and what does it mean for the dedicated users of any given world?

Here we take a look at virtual worlds on their own terms. Yes, we levy plenty of criticism, comparisons, and complaints – but the intention here is to give the virtual worlds we examine an earnest look *as they are* and as avatars experience them. This isn't an armchair rant about virtual reality; this work comes from spending time in the odd corners of virtual worlds, thinking about those worlds in terms of their information dynamics, and reporting discoveries with an eye toward improving information service in virtual worlds, in the real world, and in the coming world of augmented realities.

Our theoretical moorings

Even as information and media professionals have to be more concerned with pragmatics and practice than with abstraction and metaphor, we can't just gloss over the history and theory. Indeed, theoretical views from the social sciences in particular can help us to get our bearings and to make sense of things as we try to move forward within virtual realities. I am not concerned here about supporting any particular theoretical view as the one main or most important for understanding all the phenomenon associated with virtual worlds; but I will present a few of those that I believe to be the most relevant. Sometimes we will reference them in light of a particular event in, or attribute of, a virtual world. You can work forward from that on your own, if you wish.

Jonathan Culler (2009) presents us with a view of 'theory' as genre. Literary theory in particular isn't just summary or psychology or economic digressions about the meaning of a text, but theory may use all of these things to say something new – indeed, 'works that become theory offer accounts others can use about meaning, nature and culture, the functioning of the psyche, the relations of public to private experience and of larger historical forces to individual experience' (3–5, 5). The genre of theory means that works of theory must be read, at least in part, as works *about* theory as much as they may be read as works about any particular content used as fodder to feed the Big Perspective. The book in your hands isn't a book *of* theory, but it does hope to use theory to bring some meaning to our experiences of synthesized reality. Seriously – this is much more *reportage* and policy critique than theory. But – let's talk a little theory to help us mark out points on the compass, at least.

Hyperreality

What it is: Jean Baudrillard points out that, because our experiences are mediated (or over-mediated), we live in a kind of simulation. Because of the inclusion of mediation at almost every level of experience in 'first world' lived reality, we live in a 'hyperreal' state. We have increasing difficulty establishing a base-level reality, and our difficulty will increase as more aspects of life become mediated and simulated.

Why it matters here: That we are intentionally diving into fully simulated worlds is startling and meaningful for anyone interested in the mediation of everyday experience. Indeed, it might serve as strong evidence for a ratcheting-up of hyperreal experiences in even the banal moments of our lives. Hyperreality forces our focus onto mediation of 'real' experiences by simulators, simulations, or even the affected agents of simulating powers. When simulation of experiences alternative to the actual lived experience of the moment pulls us out of reality, we edge into hyperreality. It may happen on a bus ride, or when responding to an e-mail, when eating supper, or when making love. That it's not just 'happening to us' but that we are in fact actively courting mediation and simulation says something about our attitude toward Real Life and awareness of any experience generally – whether real or virtual.

Baudrillard works in a field of semiotic reflection which became increasingly common in the latter half of the last century as the Boorstinian *pseudo-event* came to be a real force in economics, politics, and social psychology: people (overmediated, over advertised to) increasingly respond to signs, portends, and simulations rather than to real events in Real Life.

These concerns anticipate the popular expansion of gaming and virtual worlds, and now we live in hyperreal worlds that have made entire fictional environments out of pseudo-events, out of advertising campaigns, and out of for-profit gaming entertainments and distractions.

Consumer culture plays no small part in the development of virtual worlds, and consumer culture is a locus of the hyperreal. Celia Lury treats neighborhoods and homes as fortified spaces in which advertisements have become sort of *real*, though people's lives in them are not fully real (see *Consumer Culture*, 1996). That people's (well, consumers') very homes could become the alpha nodes of simulated and consumption-driven pseudo-realities was a startling idea – but a decade later, Douglas Rushkoff would take the issue even further.

Rushkoff, a regular and vocal media critic and commentator, begins his 2009 book *Life, Inc.* with a story about how being mugged in front of his apartment in Brooklyn, New York, on Christmas Eve revealed a corporate mentality at work in his neighborhood – the living space had become a hyperreal place where reputation, gentrification, and safety mattered only in terms of their reflection in relative real estate values.

Rushkoff's neighbors weren't happy when he posted a warning about the incident in an online forum, because that online (public) forum could affect home values . . . er, home *prices* I should say anyway (xi–xxv). Rushkoff the man had become Rushkoff *The Neighbor* – and *The Neighbor* wasn't particularly real in the same way that we might hope any random human would perceive another as real. *The Neighbor* was either a boon or a bane to the bottom line of a real estate investment – no longer a man, a human, but instead just an affective agent.

The Situationists have a place in the discussion of hyperreality, too. Guy Debord famously wrote about society as a series of spectacles (1967), and how our participation in the spectacle has only an oblique bearing on reality. The spectacle dulls some of our dearest attributes; reason is diminished as we watch the spectacle roll on. We try to keep up, try to understand it, maybe even form opinions about it – but it's only ever an engagement with a construct or a show. Again, it's engagement with a simulation – not with Real Life.

Does this increase in our truck with the hyperreal lead inevitably to a situation in which the popular masses engage in Borgmann's *hyperactivity* too? We must wonder if the business inworld is more a constant, spinning, neurotic busy-ness than a processual and purposeful set of well-considered, reasonable, and present-moment centred decisive actions. What if it's all mere bling, mere spin, glam, ping, and *holler back* that just sometimes (and maybe by happenstance) leads to money, influence, and new ways to crack math problems?

Hyperreality is a rather wide lens through which to examine these issues, because there clearly isn't just one hyperreality – various competing conceptions of the relationships between simulations and Reality have led to a complex set of multiple hyperrealities. Each different understanding of the hyperreal gives us a slightly different, and always useful, glimpse of our densely mediated Real Lives, and of the moving simulation we participate in when we go inworld.

Globalization

What it is: Arjuna Appadaurai, Zygmunt Bauman, Peter Singer, and many other philosophers, sociologists, and economists have had a lot to say about globalization over the last 20 years. Less cultural isolation and more cultural, economic, governmental, and information interdependence is the new reality we came to face in the 20th Century; in the 21st Century we'll need finer tools for making sense of these globalized flows.

Why it matters here: The idea that advanced telecommunications tools meant 'the death of distance' was an overly simple idea. Although we come face to face with globalized players (see discussion of Bauman's 'globals' and 'locals' (1998)) in virtual worlds, many virtual interactions feed back into local economies and local relationships. A deal made in an online Guild affects and directs conversation and economic choices around the supper table. Understanding the gradations and qualities of the elements of globalization help us to make better sense of what happens in virtual worlds. Globalization is a driving force of online interaction, and all virtual worlds are globalized settings.

The role of mobile phones in the developing world is a shocking example of the living capillaries connecting Real Life to less-than-real worlds (or, at least, very *differently-real* worlds) of electronic bank transfers, social-media driven, micro-lending sites, and tenuous online connections between people of different social classes in countries a world apart. Micro-lending transactions between PayPal accounts on servers in San Jose, officer's wives bank accounts in Colorado Springs, and Rwandan tinsmiths pull values, real value, know-how and skill, ethnicity, nationalism, and (post-colonial) paternal attitudes together in remixed ways.

Globalization – the interconnection of previously disparate lifeways – churns all the world's systems together, and changes them all into something new and novel. A bit of clothing merchandise for a film based on a graphic novel that references a death scene in a Bolivisión *telenovela* is more than the sum of its parts.

Gender and queering

What it is: Queer Theory holds that gender roles and gender identity are built around and through the social context in which the persons 'having' gender live, work, and communicate. It holds that girls don't necessarily or naturally like the color pink, boys don't automatically play with toy trucks, but rather that gendered behavior is built from social cues; therefore gender can be 'hacked', altered, manipulated. Gender is but one aspect, one dimension, of identity – and identity can be actively and purposefully altered. Sexuality, it follows, is also mutable. Notables in the field include Judith Butler, bell hooks, and Donna Harraway (whose work also bears on transhumanism, science and technology studies, human and animal agency, and many other fields).

Why it matters here: Sex is big business in virtual worlds. Sexual encounters (such as they are) do not always map earnestly onto the sexual identities of the people behind the avatars. Gender (and, more broadly, identity itself) is mutable in the extreme in worlds where avatars are highly customizable. The personalities one encounters in virtual worlds are *versions*, *masks*, *hacks* of the real people behind them.

Maybe these alterations are low-risk ways to experiment with alterations to the basic facets of identity, but this is also full of paradox. It may become a public performance of private concerns . . . or it may be just another way to be *fabulous* or flaming or butch. Cornelia Brunner, in suggesting a *butch-femme continuum* as a way of understanding gender complexities in games and virtual worlds, makes the point that virtual worlds 'give us a set of wonderful tools for taking apart and tinkering with the things we see around us, for imagining all the things we cannot see, and of sharing what we imagine with one another' (Kafai *et al.*, 2008: 35–45). Virtual worlds, in developing sophisticated senses of play and performance, encourage an imagining of gradations of otherness. Gender – and, more broadly *identity itself* – becomes performance and play.

McKenzie Wark provides a further bit of evidence in this direction when he posits that skin color in *The Sims 2* (along with gender, eye color, height, weight, hair-do, and so on) is arbitrary and 'mere decoration' (2007: 39). When gender identity is *accessorized* into a sort of bauble that's added or dropped depending on the needs of the social outfit, it can hardly be taken very seriously as an immutable object of personhood.

On the other hand, five minutes of chatting with random avatars in *World of Warcraft* does nothing but reinforce the idea that a core gender identity is pretty central to most everybody you meet – whether online or in the Real World. The reasoning for most avatars you might meet goes: he's a dude, yet he's playing a female Night Elf, therefore he must be gay. But then again, most avatars you meet are helmed by 12-year-olds.

If Wark is right and gender is a sort of fashion accessory inworld, then we must consider the person doing the accessorizing: is that person, when all bauble, decor, and costume has been taken away, male or female? It seems that Queer Theory, at least as it comes full circle in the play-pretend realities of virtual worlds, trends toward its own negation. If gender and sexuality are arbitrary and non-essential, then what is the actual gender of the essential person affected by these arbitrary sexual conditions?

Actor-Network Theory

What it is: Non-human actors are also social actors. If we take the whole ontology of human experience as a *social* one because its subjects are all of us individual (human) social perceivers, then any and all interactions between us and the world we interact with *are social* because we are a part of the interaction. Not only does technology mediate social engagement between humans, but technology *generates* social experiences. In stubbing your toe at the top of the escalator, the escalator itself, its designers and builders, and your own clumsy self are all the subjects of your anger. There are no non-actors within the network of social interactions. John Law, Bruno Latour, and Michel Callon all had a lot to say about these fields of agency and social interaction.

Why it matters here: We are working in, exploring, and playing with virtual realities built from a network of technological artifacts (hardware, software) that are social actors. Denying 'actor' status to anything (or any 'thing') just because it fails to *appear to be human* becomes problematic in such environments: all things in virtual worlds are partly human, partly machine, but imminently *actors* possessing agency within a social network. Processes (not just machines, people, or houseplants blogging about their soil conditions) can be actors too.

The more 'virtual' the reality becomes (or, if you like, the closer machines come to passing Turing's test) the harder it will be to tease out the human aspects from the machine, or vice-versa. Virtual worlds are stages on which we try to connect to others, but those 'others' don't necessarily need to be human (or fully human). Virtual interaction in light of Actor-Network highlights our human desire to make connections and participate in meaningful stories, but it is value-neutral about the nature of the actors with whom we do this. Which will hurt Jaron Lanier's feelings, but it's true.

Actor-Network Theory is bold. The presumption that any entanglement of any person, place, thing, or idea with any human being is a *social* entanglement and leads to social exchanges with any possible (human or non-human) interlocutor is a startling idea; virtual worlds will make great test laboratories for fine-tuning levels of human receptivity to various qualities of social actors.

And don't we already see this reality put perfectly in place inside any given virtual world? When every exchange is mediated and virtualized, we don't have the needed perspective to tell which actor or object or avatar is *human* and which is not. Glowing purple potatoes, spinning in cinnamon-colored tutus with matching topaz tiaras, may just as easily (and truly) represent a human actor as might a bouncing photograph of a guy dipping a cane pole in the mud for crawdads at his family reunion.

If any object can be a sort of *human* (read: social) object, then it's also equally possible that any object, including any human-like avatar, may be what we would normally call 'non-human' (i.e. computer programs). That means that within any given virtual world, we may or may not be dealing with human actors. God bless Alan Turing.

Intertextuality

What it is: That one text can only be read, or read to be understood, in the context of the environment of texts that came before it is a sophomore-level concept in literary circles. But in virtual worlds the effects of intertextuality are much more quickly seen and felt. A pop music event influences the development of an entire virtual platform – the aesthetic of the new world reflects the interests of the musician (as in the intersection of *Worlds.com* and David Bowie in the 1990s and early 2000s).

Why it matters here: With a large and very active population of avatars, virtual worlds quickly churn pop (and obscure) literary, musical, visual, and performance tropes into products and cultural currency. Any given performance or object in a virtual world is seated somewhere in the broad scope of the cultural 'texts' that preceded it. The rate of information exchange online and in virtual world cranks up the urgency with which anyone studying cultures in virtual worlds must understand allusions, symbols, and context.

Transhumanism

What it is: Transhumanism has strong descent lines from Queer Theory, ANT, libertarianism, and humanism. The main thrust of its concerns is that humans and the technology humans have built are headed toward a convergence of some kind. Many transhumanists hold that free people should have the right to use technology to alter their bodies, minds, and environments in whatever way they see fit (so long, often goes the caveat, as it does not impinge on any other person's rights). Transhumanism, then, may be seen as much as a political position as it is a philosophical one.

Why it matters here: Virtual worlds offer ways to model transhuman and posthuman projects, including social systems that may come after The Singularity. New convergence technologies, such as refined voice recognition software, gestural interfaces, and brain-wave control devices, have been developed specifically as tools for streamlining our psychosomatic experiences inworld. The mutability suggested by Queer

Theory and Actor-Network Theory is tied together and magnified by Transhumanism. Virtual worlds provide fictional settings to test transhuman scenarios; from personal and social reactions to grave body modification, to the dehumanizing effects (or not) of machine integration into flesh, virtual worlds can be sandboxes for proto-posthumans. The idea that virtual worlds may be the breeding grounds for a libertarian-tilted techno-social revolution should be of great interest to most cultural observers.

Nubuyoshi Terashima takes concerns about mediation and hyperreality fit squarely into transhumanist turf when he ties the blending of simulations with Real experience and the conflation of artificial intelligences with human intelligences in such blended environments (see *Hyperreality*, 2001). Terashima's work bridges the work of Baudrillard and transhumanism, because it lays out a space beyond mere 'virtual reality', which is more-or-less a simple simulation, and opens the way for a genuinely alternative experience of reality which relies on human co-evolution with technology. As John Tiffin, working with Terashima, puts it: 'A HyperWorld is not only where what is real and what is virtual interact, it is where human intelligence meets artificial intelligence.' (2001: 33). This is a clear overlap between media theory and transhumanist concerns.

Transhumanism is pointedly focused on how media (and everything else) changes on the way toward and beyond the techno-social singularity. The 'singularity' is the point at which human intelligence is bound with super-human artificial intelligences. Though the definition of singularity is described in various ways, this is an over-riding and common theme: transformation of human culture into superhuman status by way of incorporating our most advanced tools into our own (now purposeful) evolution.

It will be clear that all of these theories are important online, and indeed some have been used to make sense of hypertext or the World Wide Web for some years now (see the ties between hypertext and intertextuality in Landow's work (1994, 2006), for example, or read the general concern in ANT for social networks between people and machines). These theoretical frameworks help us make sense of the specific concerns of each virtual world we'll explore; but these few broad theories won't be our only tools – when appropriate, other modes of understanding virtual worlds will be brought in as well (I hear somebody out there holler: *Why's he not mentioned Jurgen Habermas? I've hung me whole career on Habermas . . . Show a little* love, *mate!*), so don't worry just yet. It's not like the concerns of the Marxists or Feminists, or about environment or ethnicity have been shut out. Globalization and

Situationism incorporate elements of political and economic critiques. Queer Theory, to some extent, has metabolized and obviated Feminism. Ethnicity, language, and citizenship are all concerns of globalization studies, and their impacts online (or the impact that being online has on language, etc.) is, by now, not new territory. And, again, the sketches above do not exhaust the theories that could or should be used to understand virtual worlds: they simply act as the mainmost tools for the book in hand.

Spaces and how to move in them

We normally encounter spaces with our bodies, but online and in virtual worlds (and you'll by now quickly be able to pipe up with a reminder that not all 'online' activity is work in virtual worlds) we move through implied or suggested spaces with our minds. Imagination and sensation have to be balanced carefully in order for the illusion of 'virtual' to be maintained. Our bodies remain involved, but are engaged, if you will, at a much lower level than they are when we physically stroll, dance, or swim. Sight and tactility and hearing – eyes on the animation, fingers on the mouse, ears interpreting an inworld klaxon – serve as our primary way to engage the virtual. Our physical legs and backs still matter 'online' in as much as they support the organs doing the 'real work' of seeing and clicking, but they do get relegated in the popular otaku imagination to mere 'meat' and they have been since the early days of the Web (see especially Sirius, 1996) for a documentary of the wild Internet becoming a somewhat tamer Web).

Engaging a virtual space is still very much akin to browsing the Web: we sit, we stare, we click. We blink, we shrug, we tap. The body moves little; but in the imagined space – the virtual world – we're running, whirling a sword, sharing a kiss, repairing an engine. The imagined body may be fully engaged while the 'meat' we leave sagging in a chair back in Slough atrophies in the dark. Find more on physicality and gestural engagement with information in Chapter 8.

In virtual worlds and in real life, finding information and learning how to use it is of primary importance. Information is a tool by whose use we can get the stuff we need to survive. Tracks tell us which direction the kudu walked; information turns into protein, protein into muscle, muscle repairs a shelter, shelter keeps this child dry, and the child gets well and grows strong. Information is our most important tool, because it allows us to find ways to all other tools and outcomes. Information is the meta-tool.

Running in virtual spacetime

If virtual objects, features, entities, avatars, or agents could experience space and time, perhaps they would experience it differently than we do in Real Life. When we ride an avatar, we project our sense of time onto a virtual world to make it perform in a way that's comprehensible to us. But what is virtual native time like? What would movement through a truly virtual space as a native virtual being be like?

Jack Schulze (2010) and BERG Design Consultancy offers a provocative glimpse into virtual and augmented realities as they could be 'experienced' by non-humans or human-machine hybrids in the 'Making Future Magic' project. Although 'posthumans' might be a tidier way to put this, it would also be inexact. 'Making Future Magic' makes use of flat slices of virtual 3D objects, and as each slice of the object moves across a designated space, it's photographed so that the whole 3D object can be captured *out of time* as video.

As the blog post describing the experiments puts it, they first create 'software models of three-dimensional typography, objects and animations . . . We render cross-sections of these models, like a virtual CAT scan, making a series of outlines of slices of each form. We play these back on the surface of the iPad as movies, and drag the iPad through the air to extrude shapes captured in long exposure photographs. Each 3D form is itself a single frame of a 3D animation, so each long exposure still is only a single image in a composite stop frame animation' (Schulze, 2010).

With this technique we can see floating words of light suspended above objects as metadata *cum* designer labeling, room-long cityscapes the color of television static stretched out across architectural students' worktables, and even the illusion of autonomous little virtual bots, motoring their ways across dusty floors toward some spare cellphone signal, dodging the footpaths of hungry graduate students.

The project underlines the differences between normal and fleshy time as we experience it, and the digital, pixelated, pale-blue time of entities that belong to virtual worlds. It compels us to question various and competing qualities of time.

Human beings look out of place as the digital actors move and tumble; the actors themselves look natural in their movements. Humans stare and stall and flicker in and out of digital time, and this seems to imply that time and space in virtual worlds will remain experientially out of reach for folks embodied in Real Life.

Money moves worlds

Information is bound tightly to economic realities. Movement in spaces seeking kudu meat or Linden dollars, movement either real or imagined, is always anteceded by our relationship to information. We either want new (or refined) information, or we are acting on information we have already received and understand (or think we understand).

The economies of virtual worlds and real life, then, are very tightly bound together; there is no virtual economy that does not have its origins in the economies of real life, and there are no effects of virtual exchanges that have no impact on real life. Whatever quantity of information might drive us to action with our bodies may also drive us to virtual action with our minds; we move into and through spaces because we need information. How we go about this movement, depends on the particularities of the space at hand and on what we know (or think we know) about that space.

In the broadest mode, a virtual space should be a space aiming to be less distinguishable from reality, or one that approaches a mimicry or duplication of aspects of real life experience: it is 'virtually the same' as one's experience in four-dimensional space and time. But if it really were virtually the same (an exact duplicate, there would be no novelty or delight in it – it must be noticeably, if even only slightly, at an angle akimbo to real life to be enjoyed or reviled. Even if virtual reality is to be as fully immersive and fleshed-out as the reality of a dream, we are still meant to 'get' (even if it is a delayed realization) that the dream world is at odds, or somehow does not quite fit, with our experience of the real or the waking world. So even in the implication of sameness between real and virtual, there is a tongue-in-cheek or under-the-breath hint that the quality of life-like experience in the virtual is only nearly the same as that of real life. It's almost a sort of understated joke.

Engaging in or with a virtual space, then, is an activity that demands the participation of the imagination. Since it is (at best, perhaps) a dream-like experience, our imagination fills in the gaps that exist between fantastic moments; and, in a dream world, even a mundane action (reaching for a cup of water) has an air of the fantastic because we sense that it is not reality, but rather is, or has something to do with, another world or another kind of world. Imagination is the mortar that binds the bricks of 'virtual' experience.

Virtual worlds are worlds of the imagination, however life-like they may be. At every level, the virtual is infused with our participation through the imagination.

Virtual spaces are mysterious spaces. We know that they are like life in some way(s), but they are not life – they are something else, something unknown. It is conceivable that we could know every part of a virtual world, if that world is not a generative one, or at least that we could know all the rules of a virtual world (even a generative one). But unless it were possible to know (or to be able to experience) every possible perception of any possible avatar, it would remain impossible to know (or to experience) everything in or about any given virtual reality. As we approach a new space from a new direction, the space retreats from us; as we create a word or a name for a space, it bifurcates and roils in the experience of new users – and it remains unknowable. In this sense at least, virtual spaces are very much like real life. Virtual reality – an illusion sufficiently complex to be thought of as 'reality-like' – like real life, becomes increasingly and truly complex as we move through it and have experiences within it.

Now might be the right time to unpack a language problem. Virtual worlds, virtual spaces, virtual reality: in this text, these terms are not meant to apply strictly and only to fully immersive 'consensual hallucinations' in the way of William Gibson's cyberspace. Cyberspace, as Nitsche points out (2008: 17), 'was derived from fiction and never totally shed the element of the fictitious'. Cyberspace doesn't exist as anything other than an idea – and it's an idea that should be understood in its own proper literary and cultural contexts. It was a product of punk, *crime noir*, and of the looming existential threat of nuclear holocaust in the Cold War; it worked as a hardboiled plea for some transcendent strategy of negotiating the terrors of techno-political monoculture. Gibson's work was startling and adult. His cyberspace became synonymous with virtual reality in the popular imagination, maybe, because we appreciated that our reality was becoming something similar to The Sprawl.

In any case, 30 years later we actually find it useful to remind our readers that, though the idea of cyberspace is now old hat, we still don't actually have anything like cyberspace at all. 'Virtual worlds', then, is a kind of coarse and slightly deceptive way to get at what kinds of experiences this book investigates. The virtual worlds of *EVE Online* or *World of Warcraft* don't 'jack you in' – you're a bum on a couch, not Henry Case mind-melding with Wintermute. There is no total sensory immersion, there is no other-worldly higher plane of blue arcing data streams, and there is no more chance of meeting another conscious being in direct mind-to-mind contact online than there is any chance of doing so here on earth, beside your sweetheart, on the couch. No AI gods are going to rapture you up.

Some definitions

It's a matter of fact: we're not dealing with virtual reality as a cyberspace. Our virtual worlds are semi-imaginary spaces with built in cues for 'evocative narrative elements' (Nitsche, 2008: 3), specialized 'world physics', and (very often) social exchanges that all serve to reinforce the 'sub-creation' (in Tolkien's terms) that we build through participation.

So what is 'virtual space'? Here are some definitions:

> Virtual reality . . . applies to computer-simulated environments that can simulate places in the real world as well as in imaginary worlds. Most current virtual reality environments are primarily visual experiences, displayed either on a computer screen or through special stereoscopic displays, but some simulations include additional sensory information, such as sound through speakers or headphones. Some advanced, haptic systems now include tactile information, generally known as force feedback, in medical and gaming applications.
>
> (Wikipedia)

> Virtual Reality (VR), a technology that began in military and university laboratories more than 20 years ago, may be called Artificial Reality, Cyberspace, or Synthetic Reality. VR is a computer-created sensory experience that allows a participant to believe and barely distinguish a 'virtual' experience from a real one. VR uses computer graphics, sounds, and images to reproduce electronic versions of real-life situations . . . Virtual Reality is not a computer, but a technology that uses computerized clothing to synthesize reality.
>
> (Franchi, 1995)

> The final point of a virtual world is to dissolve the constraints of the anchored world so that we can lift anchor – not to drift aimlessly without point, but to explore anchorage in ever-new places, and, perhaps, find our way back to experience the most primitive and powerful alternative embedded in the question posed by Leibnitz – Why is there anything at all rather than nothing?
>
> (Heim, 1993)

Virtual Reality is . . . using computer technology to create a simulated, three-dimensional world that a user can manipulate and explore while feeling as if he were in that world. Scientists, theorists and engineers have designed dozens of devices and applications to achieve this goal. Opinions differ on what exactly constitutes a true VR experience, but in general it should include: Three-dimensional images that appear to be life-sized from the perspective of the user; The ability to track a user's motions, particularly his head and eye movements, and correspondingly adjust the images on the user's display to reflect the change in perspective . . .

(Strickland, 2007)

Today, 'Virtual Reality' is used in a variety of ways and often in a confusing and misleading manner. Originally, the term referred to 'Immersive Virtual Reality'. In immersive [virtual reality], the user becomes fully immersed in an artificial, three-dimensional world that is completely generated by a computer.

(Beier, 2008)

A virtual world is a genre of online community that often takes the form of a computer-based simulated environment, through which users can interact with one another and use and create objects. Virtual worlds are intended for its users to inhabit and interact, and the term today has become largely synonymous with interactive 3D virtual environments, where the users take the form of avatars visible to others graphically. These avatars are usually depicted as textual, two-dimensional, or three-dimensional graphical representations, although other forms are possible (auditory and touch sensations for example). Some, but not all, virtual worlds allow for multiple users.

(Wikipedia)

We are speaking about a technology that uses computerized clothing to synthesize shared reality. It recreates our relationship with the physical world in a new plane, no more, no less. It doesn't affect the subjective world; it doesn't have anything to do directly with what's going on inside your brain. It only has to do with what your sense organs perceive. The physical world, the thing on the other side of your sense organs, is received through these five holes, the eyes, and the ears, and the nose, and the mouth, and the skin. They're not holes, actually, and there are many more senses than five but that's the old model, so we'll just stick with it for now.

> Before you enter the Virtual Reality you'll see a pile of clothing that you have to put on in order to perceive a different world than the physical world. The clothing consists of mostly a pair of glasses and a pair of gloves. Exactly what clothing there will be it's too early to say because there are a lot of different variations that are possible and it's really too early to predict which will be the most popular ones. A minimal kind of Virtual Reality outfit would have a pair of glasses and a glove that you put on.
>
> The glasses allow you to perceive the visual world of Virtual Reality.
>
> Instead of having transparent lenses, they have visual displays that are rather like small three-dimensional televisions. They're much more sophisticated than small televisions, of course, because they have to present a three-dimensional world to you that's convincing, and there's some technology involved in accomplishing that, but that's a good metaphor. When you put them on you suddenly see a world that surrounds you – you see the virtual world. It's fully three-dimensional and it surrounds you, and as you move your head to look around, the images that you see inside the eye glasses are shifted in such a way that an illusion is created that while you're moving around the virtual world is standing still.
>
> The images come from a very powerful special computer, which I like to call the Home Reality Engine. It will be sitting there in your room and will plug into the phone outlet . . .
>
> (Lanier, 1989)

And, in some length, a definition of virtual reality's close cousin, cyberspace:

> Cyberspace is the electronic medium of computer networks, in which online communication takes place. It is readily identified with the interconnected information technology required to achieve the wide range of system capabilities associated with the transport of communication and control products and services. Current technology integrates a number of capabilities (sensors, signals, connections, transmissions, processors, and controllers) sufficient to generate a virtual interactive experience accessible regardless of a geographic location.
>
> Cyberspace is the dynamic realization of electromagnetic energy through the application of communication and control technology. In pragmatic terms, operations within this global domain allow an

interdependent network of information technology infrastructures (ITI), telecommunications networks, computer processing systems, integrated sensors, system control networks, embedded processors and controllers common to global control and communications across the electro-magnetic environment. As a social experience, individuals can interact, exchange ideas, share information, provide social support, conduct business, direct actions, create artistic media, play games, engage in political discussion, and so on. The term is rooted in the science of cybernetics from the Greek κυβερνήτης (kybernētēs, steersman, governor, pilot, or rudder) and Norbert Wiener's pioneering work in electronic communication and control science, a forerunner to current information theory and computer science.

The term 'cyberspace' was first used by the cyberpunk science fiction author William Gibson, which he would later describe as an 'evocative and essentially meaningless' buzzword that could serve as a cipher for all of his cybernetic musings (see origins of the term below). Now ubiquitous, the term has become a conventional means to describe anything associated with computers, information technology, the internet and the diverse internet culture. The United States government recognizes the interconnected information technology and the interdependent network of information technology infrastructures operating across this medium as part of the US National Critical Infrastructure.

According to Chip Morningstar and F. Randall Farmer, cyberspace is defined more by the social interactions involved rather than its technical implementation. The core characteristic is that it must be an environment that consists of many participants with the ability to affect and influence each other. They derive this concept from the observation that people seek richness, complexity, and depth within a virtual world. Hence in cyberspace, the computational medium is an augmentation of the communication channel between real people.

(Wikipedia's collectivist definition, as of September 2010).

Here, 'virtual reality', 'virtual world', and 'virtual space' will all be used synonymously to mean a complex and artificial immersive social environment. Let me break that down:

Complex and artificial – because the world must begin to approach a believable alternative to our own reality. Pong is not complex enough for players to begin to be transported to a paradise of perpetual tennis – and it probably never was, though the arguments mapping exactly when and which games did begin to approach sufficient complexity to be considered 'virtual reality', are still being hammered out. Was Pong a virtual world the first time it was played, back in the early 1970s? It is an artificial world because we access it through artificial (engineered, rendered, built) tools. We cannot create the kinds of virtual worlds that we talk about in this book with twigs and ochre and river pebbles – though it is worth noting that live action and table top role-playing games (see *Vampire: The Masquerade*, *Dungeons & Dragons*, *GURPs*, etc.) deserve their own separate discussions as alternative, hyper-, or virtual realities after a fashion, because they are shared and co-created fictional worlds (Wardrip-Fruin, 2004) contains some interesting discussions of role playing – some of which I reference later; see also the many excellent discussions about strategy, board, and role-playing games by Scott Nicholson.

Here we're talking about electronically generated environments that, because they are sufficiently complex environments, become *immersive*. They become so engrossing that we somehow forget or somehow disregard the fact that our meat is still in the day's work clothes. We forget, or we disregard, the windchimes ringing on the back patio: we're convincingly, though temporarily, transported to another world. Immersion means deep attention. We pay attention when we're interested.

Finally, these are often *social spaces*. That's the 'massively-multi-player' part of MMORPGs or MMORPWs or MUDs, etc. Other people use the Internet to communicate within an imagined space, and when you play in that space you're playing with (or at least alongside) other people. It's possible that you're inworld alone, though; it's still usually a social space for a number of reasons. The environment you move through was imagined, designed, and 'built' by other people or by groups or associations. Traces of others remain in the environment as you move through it and use it. Even if we take it to be the case that sometimes one finds herself absolutely alone in a virtual world – let's say she's just built an entirely new virtual world but it hasn't yet gone online – the dynamic exchanges between the technology used to build the world and the world's builder may in itself constitute a closed yet self-referential social network (Actor–Network Theory would make such a case).

Now we can quibble as to whether any of the example worlds we work through in this text are or are not sufficiently 'social', 'artificial', 'complex', or 'immersive', but we'll proceed with this working definition regardless. For example *The Sims* played on player consoles (i.e. home use with the PlayStation 2) would present some real problems in terms of the 'social' dimension, were it not for the fact that console games are often played with others in real time (in the same room, grabbing from the same bowl of crisps, sitting on the same stained rug, etc.), and also are now beginning (as with PS3) to allow players live and immersive online play. On the other hand, to suggest that sitting alone in a dark room is not social when a player may be typing love graffiti as a tattoo on somebody's avatar's neck, or plotting a strike against a mining colony on Mars with dozens of other gamers . . . would seem off the mark, too.

So reading one of those 'Confessions of a Shopaholic' books isn't, herein, thought of as an entry to a virtual world – but a game of *Sims* is. A guided meditation at your yoga studio isn't virtual reality – but a round of Wii Fit Yoga is. An all-night session of *Dungeons & Dragons* (dice clattering, cheeto-orange thumbs staining the Expanded Psionics Handbook, open tallboys of Red Dog going flat in the wee watches of the night) isn't an all-night movement through a virtual space – but a session of *Guild Wars* is.

2

Types of virtual worlds

Abstract: Virtual worlds can be game spaces, experimental modeling spaces, and other types of spaces. Games come in many genres, and also can be divided by types of aesthetic and interface qualities. Understanding the particularities of virtual worlds is important for information professionals.

Key words: games, perspective, aesthetics, genre, models, simulation.

Games

Games are the most common kind of virtual worlds, and for many good reasons. Games make money. Games have drama. Games are a way to gain cred, reputation, and to improve social standing amongst other gamers. Games are fun.

But as David Parlett puts it in his excellent *Oxford History of Games*: 'Play validates itself. Its purpose and value are intrinsic. True games serve no conscious practical purpose beyond that of sastisfying an urge to play which is sometimes regarded as an instinct.' Parlett quotes James Carse: 'he who *must* play cannot truly *play*.' If games are played for money, for reputation, for any of the rest, then all of those things are secondary to *fun*. And, in that case, maybe they aren't even *games* any more.

Information professionals who want to serve in game worlds have to meet the players 'where they're at' as they say: Are your inworld patrons there to make money in a virtual economy? To do sociology research? Or just to have fun?

Whatever their reasons for being inworld, an understanding of their motivations can improve relations between those of us offering services and those we are trying to serve. We don't want to go around killing buzzes, and we definitely don't want inworld patrons to run when they see our approach.

On the other hand, if we're nothing but flip and glib and witty toward patrons trying to turn a virtual dollar or develop virtual real estate, we will soon be seen as light-weight dilettantes flitting around for fun . . . when we could be very valuably doing real work for serious-minded people.

Knowing your community, again and again, is vital.

Edward Castronova spends some time working to equate games to virtual worlds. Citing numbers of players of games and numbers of subscribers to virtual worlds, Castronova soon tallies a number upwards of 30 million of active online gamers (figuring, as he was, with 2006–2007 data). But the numbers of players of world-like (immense, immersive) digital games (whether or not those games are *in fact* virtual worlds) is much, much larger; upwards of 20+ million copies of Grand Theft Auto games have been sold, 20+ million copies of the Lego Star Wars, etc. The success of the Halo series has suggested to some that video game development studios could become more financially successful and culturally influential than film studios. In any case, Castronova goes on to suggest the term 'synthetic worlds' for a rough conflation of both digital games and virtual worlds. 'Synthetic worlds are the most dynamic and energetic part of the entire digital games sector. According to the Entertainment Software Association, 19 percent of frequent gamers said they played online games in 2000; by 2006, the percentage had risen to 44 percent. Single-player gaming remains as fun as always, but it is not being treated as the future of the industry. Rather, recent developments suggest that all games are going to go online within a very few years. And when they do, they will all acquire a social dimension' (2007: 35). So, even if games and worlds aren't the same now, he suggests, they shortly will be.

I bring up Castronova's point neither to agree with it, nor to critique it on any particular front; but one must wonder if the conflation of all immersive digital game-like or world-like media into a single treatment (synthetic worlds) is useful. Clearly Castronova is right in his observations about the movement of console games into social dimensions. XBox and Wii have made what was once a private home daliance into a massively multi-player online experience – your console is another gateway into synthetic worlds. But the dilineation of game types, and of different qualities of experiences in virtual worlds demands new words, new categories, new ontological schema. To push all of this together into one lump, as if it were all always destined to become the same kind of thing, seems unfair to the real subtleties of the experiences of gamers and those who take up time in non-game virtual worlds.

Jesper Juul, on the other hand, sees games and virtual worlds in quite a different light. Juul discusses the tension between fiction and games, and criticizes too strong or strident a demarcation between one and the other (contesting, by the way, his own previous positions on the subject).

> In video game studies, the denial of fiction is an alluring position . . . based on a simple recurring argument that tends to follow this pattern:
>
> 1. Rules are what make a game a game.
> 2. Fiction is incidental to whether something is a game.
> 3. A game can be interesting without fiction.
> 4. A game with an interesting fictional world can be a terrible game.
> 5. Therefore, fiction in games is unimportant.
>
> Though the conclusion is tempting, it is also false
>
> (2005: 13).

He goes on to show how a disregard for the fictional elements of a game brings an incomplete understanding of games. A disregard for narratology in favor of ludology, in the game studies lingo, unfairly denies the importance of *story* in game worlds. Story is tied tightly to games, whether in the rigid parameters of a *progression* game or in the sometimes playful (and sometimes absurd) unfolding of an *emergence* game (195). The two (rules on one hand, fiction on the other) cannot really be pulled apart in games, unless we're talking about the grayest sorts of games imaginable.

Even board games – such as chess – that are very rule-based, imply *story*: chess has characters with roles (queens, rooks, pawns), positions, and levels of power. The hierarchy so absolute in the rules are toyed with, flipped off, joked about in the actual drama of the game – in the *story* of this particular checkmate, see, a lowly pawn took down a knight so that a bishop could hem in the king.

I quote from Juul again:

> While all games have rules, most video games also project a fictional world: The player controls the character; the game takes place in a city, in a jungle, or anywhere else. Such fictional game worlds, obviously, do not actually exist; they are worlds that the game presents and the player imagines.
>
> (121)

This is the tension Juul highlights between the real-ness of game rules and the fictional worlds that those rules help to build; it is perhaps a more interesting tension than that between the definitions of *games* and *worlds*.

It's too easy to conflate and confuse various game types already. There is a temptation to boil a world down to 'just one thing' in order to simplify our language about virtual worlds and immersive games. To peg *Civilization* as a 'Sim Game' is to leave out discussion of its genre and its gameplay. That is, if we were to shorthand *Civilization* as a simulation-type game without further discussion, we miss the other dimensions that matter so much in player experience: it's an alternative history simulation with elements of fantasy and science fiction that has very complex controls in a mainly bird's eye view (third-person) map-board world.

It's useful, then, to see games in terms of a matrix that works in at least three basic dimensions: genre, gametype, and gameplay.

Genres may be loose and multiple; that is, a game's story could borrow tropes and aesthetic cues from many genres and overlap them into a single experience. A science fiction world may borrow elements of a western (as Jos Whedon's *Firefly* series and the film *Serenity* did), a western may borrow science fiction elements to make a type of steampunk, or a romance can borrow from the fantasy genre (as do countless manga series). When we talk about genre, we're talking about these rough but recognizable categories that allow players to know what kind of world and what kind of story they will participate in ('I like detective stories' or 'I want to play a zombie game').

'Gametype' has to do with the overall structure of the game experience, and it, too, is technically a genre (a type of type); gametype, for our purposes, is distinct from how we use genre, because gametype is aesthetic or trope neutral. The overall structure may be a pure abstract strategy game, a simulation type of game, a level-based action game, a first-person fighting game, a tactical tower-defense, a 'sandbox' world with player-organized goals and adventures, a puzzle, or a role-playing game (etc.).

'Gameplay' is best understood as the moment-by-moment experience of playing the game – from what perspective is the game world most often engaged with? Are you moving an avatar through a virtual world, or are you clicking icons to make macro-level changes to a community or environment? Do you fly the airplane with a joystick while carefully tracking altimeter changes, or do you have to click the 'enter' key over and over again to land a roundhouse kick on a troll's jaw? The minute and specific details of how a gamer interacts with the computer, and how (or if) her avatar interacts with the game world all build up the experienced gameplay.

These three dimensions act as a way to 'rough out' games and situate them in relation to each other.

Detailing all the varieties of genres and sub-genres would take a lot of time, and (though plenty interesting!) wouldn't be all that useful here. After all, genres and their variations can be understood well enough through other stories in other media – there is nothing implicit in the 'gameness' of a military action game that makes it unintelligible in comparison to a military action documentary or novel. It will prove useful, however, to detail gametypes and some of the major issues in gameplay.

Gametypes

Gametype, like genre, is complex. But not so complex that we can't begin to give it a little language and see what it's made of. Many varieties of gametype exist and are in use in popular and obscure games – but as we explore the issue of virtual worlds, it's only really the gametypes that use some form of 'interactive fiction' that concern us. Interactive fiction 'simulates a world, understands natural-language text input from an interactor and provides a textual reply based on events in the world' (Montfort in Wardrip-Fruin, 2004: 316). This world-building effect of interactive fiction, and the fact that it points toward some subjective actor and his experience as a player in the world or a character in a story, is what makes the gametypes of virtual worlds distinct from other games (or non-worlds).

Simulation games are a broad category of games that allow players to tinker with lives, ecosystems, cities, or worlds. Will Wright's *SimCity*, first published in 1989, is the classic 'city-building' simulation that gave rise to so many riffs and re-imaginings of what games could become by using world simulation. Sid Meier's *Civilization*, which was conceptually similar to SimCity and used similar gameplay elements, was under development when SimCity appeared in 1989 (Edwards, 2007). These games are part of the 'construction and management simulation games' subgenre of 'simulation games' (see especially Wolf, 2002: Ch. 6) and are in Juul's 'emergence' category.

In these games, your work is to *build stuff*. It might be a city or a civilization, as above, it could be a species (then cities and civilizations – as in *Spore*), it could be an amusement park, a planet, an ant colony, or a medieval economy. It takes a high level of interest in managerial tasks to play these well. Players do well to be very interested in the minutiae and meanings of lots of little knobs and switches inworld (click *this* icon for water infrastructure, but then watch as it folds out into a tree of choices including *new pipes, well stations, dams, wind pumps*, and *water treatment plants*, for instance). These are sometimes called 'god games' because the player, within a set of rules maintaining a basic consistency in inworld physics and dynamics, gets to do whatever she wants. Sometimes even the 'rules' governing interactions and economics get tossed out with freely available cheat codes. You say you don't have enough cash to build that superhighway connecting two island cities? Check again.

Role-playing games are usually both dramatic and highly subjective, and are wide open for all kinds of experiences. The great appeal of role-playing games is that the variety of situations a player may find herself in is only limited by the imaginations of those playing the game together. In many cases, you 'make it up as you go along', riffing and improvising off each other's actions and ideas. There has to be balance between structure/ narrative and improvisation for role playing to work well and be fun. The tension between the various ways individuals imagine situations in role-playing games (and I'm thinking of tabletop games in particular here) gives rise to the need for rules and systems.

Will Hindmarch puts it very well in his tidy and refreshing essay (in Wardrip-Fruin, 2007) on the *Vampire* series from White Wolf Publishing: 'Until . . . details are challenged, and it becomes necessary for all of the players to agree on them for the sake of the action, each player's mental image goes untransmitted and exists only in their own imaginary space.' But when the players are called on to imagine a particular kind of detail (the cemetery has short, weedy headstones rather than tall mausoleums), mechanics are in place to level out the co-imagined world and make it conform to the necessities of the narrative. 'The rules represent a kind of social contract between the players. If a player chooses to ignore a penalty or injury to her character that comes from the game world, then she is plainly not participating in the game. If one player declares, "I shot you!" another player cannot simply insist, "You missed!" unless the dice back her up' (51).

As in life, the tensions are what make it interesting. In virtual game worlds, the tensions surrounding the negotiation of imagined spaces are removed – the world simply *is* as it *is*, and all players must conform uniformly and instantly to the objective reality of the world. This is a loss for several reasons, not the least of which is that individual gamers are towed into an unflexible and conformity-enforcing communal experience. In tabletop gaming the *exercise* of the individual's imagination in building a world and its characters is of primary importance and pleasure, and the free exercise of imagination and will empower individuals. There is no enforced conformity – only negotiations of will and imagination when the story demands resolutions for conflicts.

Action/Shooter games, though they may be set within complex and sophisticated worlds of various genres, mostly center on the activity of fighting. A fantasy action game may offer a sorceress throwing lightning at orcs, or a ranger fighting forest bandits with short sword and daggers; a science fiction take may offer a gunned-up cyborg; etc. The major concern of action and shooter games is the individual's performance of critical (extreme, life-or-death, etc.) tasks in the way of delivering some broader good or goal. Even in games of shared fighting performance (think of team play in the *Call of Duty* series), the individual's role within the team is the locus of all action.

Social action in shooter games is about the individuals – it's about the trees, not the forests. And the individuality of the experience is important as understood for any individual gamer's avatar inworld, but also for the individual experience of the gamer herself. Couch, popcorn, Icehouse beer (Plank Road Brewery, if you please) is all well and good – but the execution of the avatar's 400-yard shot to the gas-tank of a warlord's sedan from the shade-side of an abandoned minaret? That's something done by a single player; it's her muscle-memory, her tactile smarts, her grokking of virtual space-time that lets the shot fly true. It's an individual's victory if the car goes boom, even as hidden flanks of special operators roll in low and hard to secure the site and verify the kill. This is what passes for glory.

Vehicle-centric games, sports games (excepting those that edge into serious simulation – see above), 'first-person shooters', beat 'em ups, and 2D fighters (*Street Fighter*-style fighting games after the Capcom styles): they all value tactics above strategy, and they all depend on decisions made quickly. You go, you do, you move, you shoot. Roll, twist, snag: trick it out. Action and shooter games let us vicariously do damage, run amok, blow up aliens, steal cars, blow up cops, blow up priests, and blow up ourselves. The value of this last is not easily overstated: the reckless fun of running your Williams FW07 into a gaudy billboard at the Fuji International Speedway just for the hell of it . . . well, if you like that kind of thing, it *really does satisfy*.

Other gametypes are surely worth mentioning, and there are plenty of others. Some we'll miss mentioning due to our boredom with their tropes or their lack of *weight and heft*. Puzzle games abound, for instance. You can do math puzzles or play backgammon 24/7, if you like. Tower Defense games are good. Also, the *Risk*-like *Kdice* (and similar variants) is unlike other gametypes – it asks the player to work both tactically and strategically in her defense against (and attack of) other territorial interests. There are word game puzzles. A certain kind of 'physics' or 'engineering' drag-and-drop puzzle is on the rise at sites like Candystand and Kongregate. There are visual match-ups, spot-the-differences, and music games, too. Etc.

But it's the simulations, role-playing games, and action/shooter games that represent the three categories that cover the most games, and they establish the three broad gametypes to which genre and gameplay issues relate so that an immersive gaming experience may instantiate for the player at hand. It's in these games that any given player is most likely to have substantial meaningful experiences via his or her avatars.

Issues in gameplay are many, varied, and complex; many books have spent many pages working out the details of gameplay experiences and what these experiences mean (see Bibliography for some suggestions to begin with. Go read Nitsche (2008) for his full-on dive into gameplay: he does a much better job than I can do here. I'll have to simplify all these complex issues into three major categories: perspective, aesthetics, and interface 'clickiness'.

Perspective, aesthetics, clickiness

Perspective immediately establishes the degree to which a game will be *visceral* by sending cues that the business of the game will be at a removed and filtered distance (a third-person perspective), or by communicating avatar-level personal immersion (first-person movement through a world); there is a spectrum of perspective and immersion. A far-removed and 'god-like' perspective (very common in simulation games) generally decreases the *pathos* and drama at work in the game, as our identification with particular individuals decreases. Simulation games and third-person, god-like, perspectives allow us into other kinds of drama and fun, such as village-level or planet-level successes and failures – but the value f each individual character, and the choices she has to make to succeed or even survive, drops of dramatically the further out our perspective zooms.

Second-person perspectives, as in *beat 'em ups*, let you see a wide camera shot of the world around your avatar (though the characters in such games are usually very rudimentary and would not normally be thought of as avatars – not customizable, not elegant, not machinimatic), and thereby lends a sense of 'control at a distance'. The 2D fighting games that were the heirs to beat 'em ups (Capcom's series of *Street Fighter* games being the premier exemplars of 2Ds) are more immersive, more visceral, because 'your character' or your avatar is much larger on the screen, responds even to small and subtle joystick and button movements, and is much more fully drawn, detailed, colored, and animated.

In first-person perspective, the shininess of your avatar drops away. It's the *world* that's on display, now. You move through a virtual environment in four dimensions (space plus time), seeing things from the height of your avatar, and seeing the world lurch forth according to the pace of your avatar's gait.

This last points us toward the next major issue in gameplay – aesthetics. The 'look' or 'the visuals' or 'the graphics' of a game all work to make it attractive to gamers, though look, visuals, and graphics are different things.

Look may have to do with a wide range of visual style, and is the closest to a pure concern for aesthetic. Look means design, repetition of visual elements, and even the *beauty* of characters, buildings, objects, backgrounds, maps, and other features in the game. When we respond to the question *does it look good?* – it's the game's 'look' that we refer to in order to answer; however, we cannot say a game consistently looks good without considering other aesthetic aspects such as 'visuals' and 'graphics' – these aren't static games, after all, and the moving or animated elements fit with 'look' to create our overall aesthetic impression.

Visuals have to do with patterns of movement, and how those patterns affect the experience of the game. Visuals have direct impact on, and are directly impacted by, both *perspective* and *aesthetic* concerns. Visuals use aesthetic elements to communicate tone, mood, and spaces to the player. We can talk about visuals in terms of Ching's definitions for 'visual properties'. Nitsche (2008) revisits Ching's 1979 work on architecture, quoting the key visual properties: 'shape/size/color/texture/position/orientation/visual intertia . . . The resulting combinations of properties are manifold . . .' Nitsche goes on to define Ching's take on visual axes, symmetry, hierarchy (spatial cues about the importance of objects), repetition, and others (Ching, 1979; Nitsche, 2008: 163).

How does the 'camera' move, and how does changes in perspective (smooth, wavy, bumpy, wiggly transitions from place to place in the point of view) repeat or establish 'rhythm' in concert with a game's color palette, or its contrast, or its line-widths? All are concerns of the visuals of the game. Ikeno's work on Street Fighter IV repeated hand-drawn and calligraphic elements to such an extent that the player is spattered with 'ink smudges and ink sprays during the fights' ('Visuals', 2010). Giddings and Kennedy, in their wonderful study focusing on Lego Star Wars, demonstrate the interconnectedness of visual elements (including what we would here call 'visuals') to the whole experience of playing video games: 'Video games as screen media texts offer visual pleasures; the attractions of [games] are inseparable from the beauty of their graphics' (Giddings & Kennedy in Swalwell, 2008). They also do a darn good job of applying Actor-Network Theory to games, as it happens.

'Clickiness' can gauge how much manual interaction the game requires. Lots of 'clicks', button taps, joystick rolls, or punching of arrow keys: all indicate a high clickiness level. Some games just need a little push now and then – they've got much less clickiness, more of a 'low key' interface.

But clickiness also happens virtually, ingame or inworld. The amount of controls necessary to operate Sid Meier's *Civilization* (for example, or EA's *Lord of the Rings: Battle for Middle Earth*, or *EVE ONLINE*, or any number of other complex games) is extraordinary, but the multitude of controls are virtual, are inworld, and one accesses these myriad and many controls through very simple physical gestures on the computer keyboard or console controller. The complexity of clickiness is relative. *Sims: Bustin' Out* seems kinda complicated to me, but my wife finds it breezy. Easy. We both grok most of the *Sim City* games, but neither of us cottons much to *SimCity Societies:* the number of controls or in-game knobs isn't that tough, but the gameplay so slows and muddies response, that accessing the controls turns into a big bother. Thereby the clickiness is inordinate and overbearing in a *bad* way.

If the clickiness isn't qualitatively bad (read: annoying, slow, or *dumb*) then the amount of buttons and controls, or their scarcity isn't an indicator, in itself, of any positive or negative value. *Good* clickiness (in high or low levels) appeals to different kinds of players in different ways, and for different reasons. Sometimes a small and elegant thumb gesture in a broader context of quiet and occasional down-taps *works just right*. But at other times, a player may want a million and two variations on autumn and spring tones in a makeover of their quarter-extraterrestrial femme Sim. Clickiness, done right, can enhance enjoyment. Clickiness, done stupid, drags down the game, increases the time needed for the banal, and builds resentment for the game by the players.

Some games have various, maybe even fractaling, genres and genre-splices. A game in any genre has also some position in the matrix of gametype, gameplay, and interface (clickiness). And we won't even address the narrative analyses or *cyberdramatic* criticism of games that becomes possible when video game screen is read as 'text' (Giddings & Kennedy mentions, but see especially Murray, Loyall, Perlin, and Wright in Wardrip-Fruin, 2004). But from this position, you can see that the variations of experience in games are sufficiently numerous to be effectively infinite.

I want next to say something about the general properties of non-game virtual spaces, and it's best to do so in the context of finite and infinite games; some of the games mentioned above are finite, and some are infinite (*finite* and *infinite* in the sense Carse uses them). Non-game spaces can contain games (a dance off in *Second Life* – somebody dances best and wins the night), and they can contain both finite and infinite types of games. The dancing contest may be finite (6–8 PM GMT, Tuesday night, one night only! Best Dancer gets an inworld teeshirt designed by M.I.A.!!!), but it could be modified to become infinite (show up in this spot every Tuesday night and dance. Learn new dance moves. Use them during the week at inappropriate times. Report back to fellow dancers. Each week, the teller of the best 'dance story' will get to change the color of the sky.).

Which is to say that, because these worlds can contain finite and infinite games, and because they can contain no games at all (you can just sit on top of a virtual building and smoke a virtual pipe, listening to the mating songs of pteradactyls), they are a new category of thing in human experience. In non-game worlds there is no over-arching narrative driven by plot or particular characters. There is no time limit. There is no particular thing that anyone *has* to do. This is something totally new, and we humans don't yet seem to know really what to do with this new kind of space.

Non-games

Non-game spaces, though called 'non-game' because they are open worlds without any set agendas or goals (and very low levels of intrinsic drama or tension), may themselves be thought of in some sense as infinite games. A 'non-game' space as an 'infinite game'? I say so because the structures of the world can be played with, indeed, are *meant* to be played with, in such a way that new games and new dramas can be generated within the world. There's nothing you *have to do* in *Second Life*; but if you build on an island, you're likely to have inworld neighbors. When you have neighbors (when other agents or actors exist to interact with), games develop. The rules of development can become a kind of game, too. Knowledge of the Linden Scripting Language (LSL) allows users to build an inworld version of almost anything they might imagine. Script your own clothes, hairstyles, tables, chairs, vehicles, or buildings. This sort of 'open play' through unstructured virtual design and building *is* the infinite game. So this, as I call it, *non-game world*, has an infinite game built into its very foundations – and this is what allows its users to come and just *be* without having to *play* at all if they don't wish to.

Non-game spaces, and we settle on that term for them despite the complications spelled out above, do lots of different 'non-game things'. A game space (think *Guild Wars, Evony*, or *Monkey Tower Defense*) is designed for playing games; non-game spaces are open, at least in theory, to the simulation or virtualization of all other kinds of human endeavors. That's why we find educational, spiritual, and even medical worlds (or spaces within worlds) like the Starlight Foundation's *Starbright World*, which provides an exclusive virtual world for 'sick teens and their teen siblings' to connect with each other and share their reflections and experiences.

As Lori Bell's analysis suggests (Evans, 2009: 163–164), we come to understand information in more genuinely creative ways when we work within four-dimensional virtual worlds. This may be because we're using information about the modeled or virtual world in novel ways – and ways different from other daily uses (watching videos, reading text, playing two-dimensional games, etc.) This educational component, which is (perhaps) inherent in the experience of the virtual, presents us with a set of meta-models. Whatever we want to do or want to learn about, we can experience directly and create with code. Who was it that said virtual worlds themselves act as meta-models and as meta-media?

Of all the virtual worlds, *Second Life* is the usual media darling, the most common world to get and keep the attention of the people who have lots of money. Universities build campuses, professors hold class, and authors meet their readers inworld. NOAA offers plane rides through hurricanes, aging goth ladies listen to *My Bloody Valentine* in the black towers of Mãebaleia, and cowboys fire at flying smileys down by Ahern's Shooting Gallery. This sort of stuff isn't nearly so likely to happen in *Worlds* (*Worlds.com*), *Guild Wars, Active Worlds*, or *World of Warcraft*; some of the reasons are technical (*Second Life* allows building and development in ways that other worlds aren't able to), but some of this just has to do with accidents of money, media attention, and recent history. You might say that *Second Life* came along at just the right time . . . and *Worlds* came along 10 years too early. Google's *Lively*? Amongst other problems, it came along way too late.

Virtual Earth (Microsoft's and Google Earth) and even *SketchUp*, the popular CAD/modelling program that Google bought in 2006, deserve a brief mention. *SketchUp*, though hardly qualifying as a social space, it is at least complex, artificial, and immersive. In it, we can build virtual objects – homes, machines, landscapes – and we can even pull these 3D models out of the program and 'print' them into Real Life via 3D printing tools like CADspan. Virtual earth platforms bind terrain data and satellite imagery with the usual GIS elements (place names, roads, political boundaries), but in the case of .kml and .kmz files, this effort goes much further. The open API of Google Earth for example, allows independent developers to create mapping data that may range from military statistics (where and how many IEDs exploded within 1 kilometer of Karz, Kandahar, Afghanistan in 2010?) to cultural and economic data (which cities in Germany see the highest sales for TOKYOPOP manga titles?). This turns out models that are complex, artificial, and immersive. Again – not particularly social. It's a singular and solitary experience: zooming over the farmlands bordering the De Soto National Forest, dipping down into frost pockets and creek beds, rising again to bank left around the east face of a bare hill, red-brown with pine straw.

We can talk Revit, Marionette, ArcView, Pro-E, RenderMan, AutoCAD, and other specialized programs like VISIBLE, too. These begin to bleed out of the realm of virtual *worlds* and into very specialized tools that begin to allow us *world-building* abilities instead of just *world-wandering* abilities. Sure, *Second Life* gives its users the Linden Scripting Language to build stuff inworld; but LSL can't hold a candle to serious engineering software in terms of technical detail or its ability for creative expression. And besides, LSL isn't mean to do the same stuff as Pro-E. They are not competitors.

Non-game virtual worlds and design systems, though usually less social and less immersive than game spaces, present us with very serious tool sets for modeling all kinds of processes, spaces, interactions, and technologies.

Not all of these worlds and spaces fall into a for-profit mold. OpenSimulator is an opensource development package for virtual worlds. To give you an idea of their 'vibe', their main site, *opensimulator.org,* is done on MediaWiki. At the top of the website it says:

> OpenSimulator is a 3D Application Server. It can be used to create a virtual environment (or world) that can be accessed through a variety of clients, on multiple protocols. OpenSimulator allows you to develop your environment using the technologies you feel work best – we've designed the software to be easily extendable through loadable modules to build completely custom configurations.

> OpenSimulator is released under a BSD License, making it both open source, and commercially friendly to embed in products. Out of the box, OpenSimulator can be used to simulate a virtual environment similar to *Second Life* (including client compatibility). Other environments, protocols and features are supported via add on modules. For a list of available modules check out our forge site.

The OpenSimulator page at Forge gives us a bit more:

> OpenSim Forge provides free hosting for Open Source projects related to the main opensim project (such as alternative gridservers, plugins and region modules, etc). To apply for space for your project, create a user account, then apply from the control panel.

We're talking real *free-as-in-freedom*, here.

Forterra System's, by contrast, is all corporate, all contract, and all profit. There's no *free-as-in-beer* here, and their spin on virtual world code is all proprietary and for profit-centered applications. Their RemoteOperations(TM) application for virtual worlds had its own brochure (indeed, Forterra had their own website before being purchased by SAIC in 2010), which lauded the necessity of virtual environments for contingency operations in the face of biological disasters:

> Organizations today are facing a full-blown flu pandemic due to the widespread outbreak of influenza caused by the H1N1 (Swine Flu) virus that has reportedly caused over 1000 deaths in the US so far this year. According to the Centers for Disease Control, the 'Influenza is thought to spread mainly person-to-person through coughing or sneezing of infected people'. When the H1N1 virus touches your organization, the first reaction of employees will be to strongly discourage those that have been or may be infected by the virus from coming to the office . . .
>
> What do you do now? How can you hold your project together while preventing further the spread of this virus? If your organization has not already faced this or a similar scenario, it will. And one management response will be to forbid employees from coming to the office.
>
> Forterra Systems, a leader in private virtual world technology, is offering RemoteOperations™, a collaboration and communication solution to help overcome these obstacles and ensure organizations can continue to function at high levels despite the current challenges.

> Based on distributed, on-line 3D internet technology, Remote Operations allows participants to work from remote locations just as they would in person

Forterra was timely with the offer of this service (too timely, in fact – this may have sold some code in 2009, but by 2010 'Swine Flu' reminded us only of an overblown overreaction by what would soon come to be seen by many as an overbearing government), but there's a problem here. Common sense would suggest that if you're too sick to come into work – because you're struck with the chills, aching, and body-wracking coughs of influenza – you're also *too sick to work*. It seems assumed that somehow, because the (real) work is conducted at a virtual site, the work itself becomes even less taxing than serious play. Folks are expected to *nut up*, if you will, and show up online. Forterra provides a tool by which that may continue to happen. Of course, it comes at a price; and the price is much higher than either *Second Life* or OpenSimulator. Are we then to assume that it is also somehow worth much more?

And then there's the nonprofit Starlight Foundation's virtual world, which is specifically designed as a therapeutic tool. As mentioned above, terminally ill children and teenagers can login to a social space that excludes people not in their peer group (well people of any age, and adults). In this environment, sick kids can build friendships and have exchanges that help them come to terms with their own mortality. Facing down death isn't easy for anybody – but to have to do it at 14 years old . . . Such grave matters demand a novel use of tools to see if something (anything) might ease a mind and comfort a young heart.

The same (or a similar) kind of healing, perhaps to a lesser degree, can and does take place in Web 1.0 chat rooms or old-fashioned Bulletin Board Systems. Anywhere and anyhow, people can use social software to increase interactions, people will do so to seek out an ease to their pain and a connection to one another.

From the science education orientation of NOAA in *Second Life*, to the crisis-management bent of Forterra, non-game worlds open up opportunities to do things in immersive online environments without being tied into the strictures of rule sets. Jesper Juul's work on how fiction and rules work with and against each other is notable in this context too; but it may be the case that rule-driven environments do detract from autopoietic social collaborations necessary for real work, real play, and real therapy.

3

NOObz inworld

Abstract: The initial experiences in virtual worlds mirror other types of initiation, and these experiences can be understood as analogs to rites of passage. Gender and identity impact the initiation experience. Many games include storytelling techniques to encourage the newcomer to quickly buy-in to the new world. Non-game spaces use more passive techniques, but also attempt to initiate newcomers.

Key words: initiation, stories, symbols, rites of passage.

'Ninety percent of life is showing up.'

Woody Allen

It's hard to get out of a good hot soak in the tub. It's hard to show up to work, some nights. Going to a party, if you dread it, isn't easy.

But 'showing up' inworld *is* easy. You can be who and how you want to be, to whomever, and whenever you feel like it. It's a low cost of entry, and it's not *hard* to *show up* if all you have to do is flip open a laptop and login.

Social dynamics between friends (and 'friends') complicate this simplistic position, of course. Your avatar has a crush on Avatar Y – maybe that makes the stakes of turning up at The Mixx (Isle of Miracles, *Second Life*) a bit higher than you'd normally expect from a point-and-click experience: the butterflies in your stomach are real, even if your avatar's stomach is not.

But we all have to start somewhere, to begin something, before we can have such nervy encounters. We all have to be newbies, sometimes, and we have to begin in ignorance.

In this chapter, we'll look at what life is like for the newly initiated, and what the initiation process itself is like, in virtual worlds. The focus here is on *EVE Online*, *Guild Wars*, *Runescape*, and *Second Life*. Others are mentioned, but it's the 'newbie' experience of these four worlds that we dig into here.

The rationale: Two of these worlds are free (*Runescape*, *Second Life*), and the other two cost money; two of them are in the fantasy or 'sword and sorcery' genre (*Guild Wars*, *Runescape*), and the other two are either science-fiction, or have aesthetics of and designated areas for science-fiction (*Second Life* is open, of course, to many genres); all are popular and notable. These four represent a fair balance amongst the virtual worlds we might have chosen.

A reasonable approach to the newbie experience is to focus on the *initiatory period* one experiences when first learning about these virtual worlds – when the worlds are still new and novel. Any process of initiation in the Real world is a very vulnerable time. These games, though, don't offer any formal initiations, and a major reason for this is that the idea of an individual experience is sullied by the disembodied and 'maybe, maybe not' (maybe I'm a guy from Belarus, maybe I'm a gal from Chiba City) attitude toward identity online. When joining *Second Life*, for example, I'm not required to prove who I *really am* in the same way that I need to prove my identity to get a job. And there's no need to prove any kind of spiritual individuation in the sense of essential personhood – virtual worlds aren't in the business of baptizing newcomers, having them *reborn* as a *new man* in the new world or proving their own existences (I *blank*, therefore I am). The initiation into virtual worlds is much less profound. And since you could be anyone (often all you have to prove is that you have a working e-mail address), who exactly *is it* that's joining the virtual society?

Even for the worlds that cost to join, there are layers and levels of identity play. A working bank account or credit card identity is often (but not always) required, and that information could be tied to any working e-mail address or online persona that you wish to use. Also, your avatar's identity is only tied to the banking information in a deep dark corner of the SQL database behind the scenes; other player-characters, other avatars, even other Real Life friends need not know anything about the relationship between your avatar and your workaday self.

Initiation, as Mircea Eliade (1959) tells us, is damn serious business. In *The Sacred and the Profane* he elaborates on initiation as a transition into a new state of being within our everyday and vernacular circumstances. Though focused on concerns related to religious experience and spiritual identity, these are points that extrapolate to initiation and transformation generally:

> Here we will dwell for a moment on the symbolism of 'passage' as religious man reads it in his familiar surroundings and his daily life – in his house, for example, in the paths that he takes to go to his work, in the bridges he crosses, and so on. This symbolism is present even in the structure of his habitation. As we saw, the upper opening signifies the ascending direction to heaven, the desire for transcendence. The *threshold* inside but also the possibility of passage from one zone to another . . . But it is especially the images of the *bridge* and the *narrow gate* which suggest the idea of a dangerous passage and which, for this reason, frequently occur in initiatory and funerary rituals and mythologies. Initiation, death, mystical ecstasy, absolute knowledge, 'faith' . . . are equivalent to passage from one mode of being to another and bring about a veritable ontological mutation.
>
> (Eliade, 1959: 181)

Eliade demonstrates that even in our built spaces, our homes, our gardens, our office buildings, we have echoes of dangerous and transformative rituals: we're reminded of initiation almost everywhere, subtly but constantly. If symbols of initiation are so pervasive in the daily world of coffee stains and fluorescent lights, how common might they be in our imagined *virtual* spaces?

There are important differences in the way we normally talk about the notion of initiation in Real Life and the rather pale version that shows up in virtual environments. After all, most virtual worlds provide a lite orientation to their worlds rather than a mysterious and symbol-loaded initiation. But in as much as we are transforming by becoming our avatars or allowing our avatars to represent some aspect of our Real Life, entry inworld is a metamorphosis. To join a group of similarly transformed beings in a new type of world ought to be considered as initiation.

Gendered initiation

One of the most important differences between Real Life initiation and inworld initiation, and one of the hardest to ignore, is the factor of gender.

Here we might take issue with Judith Butler's claim that there's no such thing as essential gender identity. She says that no gender-based identity exists 'behind the expressions of gender', and that the expression itself is more important than any sense of male/female identity. 'Identity is performatively constituted by the very "expressions" that are said to be its results' (1999: 33).

In virtual worlds, the perspective that gender is constructed and performed rather than inherent (see also the work of Anne Fausto-Sterling, C. J. Pascoe, and Anne Balsamo) get more mileage. The identity *problems* inherent in online communities and virtual worlds make initiation as we usually understand it – which is almost always *gendered* – decidedly de-sexed. Newbies *pick* the gender they wish to *perform* almost as lightly as they pick the colors of their garments, their beard particularities, or their shoe styles.

Yet gender isn't (can't be) obviated by virtual identities. For one thing, the person behind the avatar has a gender of some kind. For another, the avatar has its own gender; in fact, the division between genders is often more cartoonishly distinct in virtual worlds than it ever could be in Real Life (think big BIG bosoms and broad BROAD hips for the ladies; wide shoulders and grim-set jaws for the lads). There's very little that's either *fey* or *butch* in avatars, and that's true in virtual worlds that build in clear gender differences (like *Guild Wars*) as well as in worlds that allow a lot of flexibility about look and build and sexual characteristics (like *Second Life*). Even so, we see in *Second Life* a *lite* attitude toward gender because of the inherent transcience built into avatars; avatars are mutable. In this way, we see in *Second Life* something of the values reflected by Kellee Santiago in building *Cloud*, which was 'dedicated to creating an emotionally rich, age[less] and genderless game experience' (Kafai et al., 2008: 170). Queer Theory isn't equipped for Samus Aran.

Sex is fundamental to human identity (which is why Queer Theory, with its insistence on the mutability of sexual identity, is so important), and initiation universally happens to individuals who are seen either as boys or girls (for puberty rites), or as men or women (for other kinds of initiations, later life passages, joining organizations, etc.). We may except cases of physical sexual ambiguity (hermaphrodites) or 'third genders' (such as the 'two-spirit' shamans of Native American tribes).

Victor Turner takes pains to point out the differences between the male and female initiation rites of the Ndembu people of Zambia in the 1960s. 'Although both boys and girls,' he says, 'undergo initiation ceremonies, the form and purpose of the ceremonies differ widely in either case. Boys, for instance, are circumcised, but there is no cliterodectomy of girls. Boys are initiated collectively, girls individually . . .' (1967). The differences between the purposes and comportment of male and female initiations he spells out in some detail. Again, gender provides order for initiation into the full agency of adulthood.

Those symbols of initiation (the passages, the thresholds, the stairways) that Eliade reminds us run rampant at home and office? Turns out that these symbols are quite common in virtual worlds too. Next we'll examine the induction period, the initiation into a new identity, in virtual worlds in detail and see which elements inworld provide insight into the issues of initiatory symbols.

Stories and tasks

One type of initiation is one we might call 'storied'. This style of introduction can be long-winded, and if you're not interested in the genre or the characters you're seeing and hearing, it can be very tedious. On the other hand, pulling a newbie into the world with a good *story* is classic; not only is there a great story of great importance that does put the world into some kind of sense – not only that – but you can actually be a part of the struggle between historical forces and live a (virtual) life full of meaning, place, and wonder.

Guild Wars is a good example of this. When you enter the world after the character building, you're hit over the head with the tale of Ascalon and how the good king with the flaming sword needs to recruit new heroes to rout the Charr from his previously happy lands. The Charr are pretty damn spooky: they lurch around in a gray and black and brown palette, searing and stomping greenfields, their mouths spiky and wide open. So you're roped in: see the gilded monarch, faithful and ink-stained secretary at his side. They stand over a sheer Balboa drop, watching the roar and rape and razing of the capital city of Ascalon. See the trees sagging to the left, willows dropping leaves in protest at the horror. Imagine it. Nobody's happy. Cobbler shops are in flames, rat catchers are out of business, and masons are closing up and packing off to towns further west. What blacksmith wants to brain a Charr beast with his sooty tongs when he could be hammering out a horseshoe or upsetting pig for a fancy wrought gate in a county far, far away.

It pulls a player in. The sweeping camera work, the pull-backs and pans, the ruin just outside the city gates, it's all played to good effect in making a player want to do something to help. It's not yet a *duty*, because your character isn't in any kind of *allegiance* relationship to the kingdom, but it feels a little like you are already obliged to pitch in, even before you run up to get your first lead from the king's knight. Alternatively, though it has plenty of back story, *EVE Online* invites new players to imagine their role in the new world (the other side of the wormhole) but it doesn't show any real-time report of dramatic events. The story is a pace removed, and the sense is given to us that there are just too many stories to show any one of them – except the one you are about to co-create. The big events of the past that provide the current setting for *EVE Online* (the past exploration, the wormhole gate shutting down, the divisions between the major political groups) are preface to any infinite number of stories that may begin once a player is fully on board.

Second Life just plops you down in a busy social hub – no story whatsoever to buy into. And much the same is true for *Active Worlds*, and *Worlds.com*. It's like a general live chat room that has no agenda and no common draw, random strangers milling around, making comments, trying to get others to comment on their comments.

The experience of being welcomed to a new world is, if even in a half-assed way, an initiatory experience. Very efficiently, and perhaps even perfunctorily, virtual worlds fold newbies into the local culture. But then, too, it's not a careless folding – it is often quick, and sometimes it seems shallow and crude, but the design of this usually brief initiation period is deliberate and purposeful: it gets the player inducted into the ins and outs of acting inworld without much wander or lag.

Some virtual worlds are woefully minimal in the amount of attention they give to welcoming or initiation. *Active Worlds* gives zilch, for example. You drop down into a pleasant clearing hemmed in by mountains. A globe spins. You start wandering into high craggy passes and fast-flowing blue brooks. The sky is great, but there's nobody else around for miles . . . maybe thousands of miles.

EVE Online is one of the best specimens of a world that has a, shall we say, *long gestational period* for newbies. You're hit with a large amount of detailed training, and you're hit with it in the first few hours of gaming; somehow it works well, though, as the sense of urgency built into the repeated variations on spacefaring routines make for a dramatic and fun initiation into the ways and means of New Eden. At the same time, you grow *accustomed* to the manners, language, and mechanics of the game at a steady pace. Soon enough you find yourself feeling confident enough to captain your vessel into deep space and find some original trouble on your on.

Guild Wars represents a balanced approach – not as guideless and guileless as an *Active Worlds*, but not nearly so long-winded as an *EVE Online*. *Guild Wars* gives you opportunities to train up and learn more about the world in something of an easy-going and relaxed spirit. Perhaps the first-person and close second-person perspectives, combined with the genre eye-candy of castles, waterfalls, and old forests bring in a sense of greater control than that you get in *EVE Online*. *EVE Online* has your first-person view as a starship – which, though replete with pleasures of its own, lacks the warmth of ancient and grungy dudes running along a mountain path, hunting for trolls and girls and gold. The disconnect between human avatar and the tasks and perspective in *EVE Online* might be responsible for building the urgency felt in that world (you wouldn't want anything to blow up, or to press the wrong buttons, etc.).

But *Guild Wars* is a bit different. It has no single point of entry, but rather hosts a number of different initiatory experiences for each of its four campaign worlds (three campaign worlds, technically, and an 'expansion pack'). In the Eye of the North world, you enter Ascalaon as described above – as a potential hero for a failing city-state. After the dramatic entrance, things cool down *real* quickly. The Charr seem to have been beaten back for a time, and you can run and romp in the still-stout walls of Ascalon.

Guild Wars allows a new player to pick gender, variations on skin color, hair styles, clothing color, and occupation; the *occupation* is a rough lumping into character type – what *Dungeons & Dragons* might call 'character classes' – and is what other attributes, skills, and routes to advancement all hang upon.

I quote the (unattributed – though at last check, the users Tempestz, Barek, and some anonymous others had updated the section in Spring of 2010) Wikipedia entry on *Guild Wars* character creation:

> A profession is a type of class commonly found in most RPGs and is central to the gameplay in *Guild Wars*. Each profession has an array of attributes and skills that help narrow a class's proficiency in order to perform a customized role that is determined by the player. The *warrior* profession, for example, has access to the primary *Strength* attribute that increases their effectiveness and armor penetration with martial weapons, and is able to wear heavy armor providing the highest protection of all professions. *Elementalists*, on the other hand, wear less protective armor, but can use their primary *Energy Storage* attribute to give them a much greater pool of energy than other professions.
>
> *Guild Wars* also introduces the ability to choose a secondary profession, expanding the selection of attributes and skills. A character does not, however, have access to the primary attribute of

its secondary profession. A Warrior/Elementalist, therefore, is a warrior who may use spells in combat, similar to the *Spellsword* archetype from role-playing games.

There are over a thousand skills in the game that can be acquired by the character over time, but players may only use and equip up to 8 of them at any one time. This introduces levels of strategy, in which one must have a careful selection of skills that work well with one another and with teammates in order to survive.

The core professions are Warrior, Monk, Elementalist, Ranger, Necromancer and Mesmer. The Assassin and Ritualist professions are exclusive to *Guild Wars: Factions*, which can be played along with the aforementioned core professions. The Paragon and Dervish professions are exclusive to *Guild Wars: Nightfall*, and can also be played with the core professions. Unlike the other campaigns, *Guild Wars: Eye of the North* (the only expansion pack of the *Guild Wars* franchise) does not offer any new playable professions.

You'll find a few dozen other avatars running wild (most folks run, rather than walk – which is efficient and logical, but drags down the gravity of the situation and the general dignity of the place; suddenly everybody's running like it's grade-school recess time and we're all late for the fight at the monkeybars). You can tell their profession by their costume design, and you can chat with them, but Ascalon itself is relatively small, and eventually you end up where everyone else seems to be going – down at the main gate to meet Armin Saberlin or some other non-player character who gives you a quest to complete. The compass/map feature at the top of your screen always designates the direction you must go to get the next bit of information or to do the next deed in the sequence that gets you to your goals.

On your way to complete whatever task is at hand, encounters with other players (in shared spaces), with enemies and beasts, and with the landscape itself all serve as temptations to dawdle, wantonly explore, or even give up on a task altogether. This is especially true early on in one's career inworld.

Although always prodded by reminders in your Quest Log and by the Mission Map compass high in your field of sight, sometimes you really feel called to fight – letting this Fleashreaver pass by ignored on the periphery of an icy gulch just doesn't *feel right*. You've got to go get it. On the other hand, you may be enchanted by the movement of wind in tall grass on the side of a low, rolling hill. The sun sprays patterns through the limbs and red leaves of a dying oak. You just watch. For a long time, you just watch.

Floating World, *Active World*: Islands in the Net

Second Life, *Active Worlds*, and *Worlds.com* are similar in tone, especially during the early (initiatory) moments of one's experience there. The most notable aspect has to be what Warren Ellis put so well in his (best) column on *Second Life* for Reuters:

> Lots of people have had lots to say about the recent hype surrounding *Second Life*, but very few have addressed the basic experience of the world — that you're incredibly alone there. You can spend eighty percent of your time walking through immense, labyrinthine castles that no one lives in. Visit a seemingly endless string of shops with no customers.
>
> (Ellis, 2007)

A common caricature: a few hundred academics haunt these places in daylight hours, a few thousand jerkoffs and griefers haunt it by night. But the early moments of your time in one of these worlds is much like the rest of your time: as Ellis notes, it's lonely. So this may be seen as an initiation into lonely haunting.

That's not as fair to say of *Second Life* as it is of *Active Worlds* or *Worlds.com* – *Second Life*, after all, had 826,000 unique users in March 2010 (Caoili). *Active Worlds* numbers are harder to get. In 2001, there may have been 400 unique visitors per night (12,000 per month), and there are (according to *Active Worlds*' official website) over 1,000 different worlds within its universe. But any way you want to look at it, the numbers are nowhere near that of *Second Life*. *Worlds.com*, an oldie but goodie, is only discussed in any detail here for its historical importance and early novelty – it hasn't been in a position to compete for a share of the marketplace for a long time, despite the hype generated by David Bowie's prescient interest in (and unapologetic presence in) 'the first' virtual world. *Worlds.com* launched in 1994, and that was ten years too early . . . now it's trying to wrangle money out of *World of Warcraft* and *Second Life* for patent violations.

Numbers aside, the experience is very similar across all of these worlds when no one else seems to be online. You drift, you watch, and it is very ghostly. You see more action hanging out in Wal-Mart or Sainsbury's at a quarter till midnight, I guarantee.

A salient element, therefore, is the role of games; game-oriented worlds (*Runescape*, *EVE Online*, *Guild Wars*, *World of Warcraft*) are *busy* worlds. Games are popular. Games also direct players toward an orientation to the world at hand that must necessarily involve loading avatars up with discreet new information and methods for seeking information independently. These two components, the 'new info needed' and the ways to get novel information, are both required for game worlds that depend on players understanding tasks that progress the narrative, the drama, or the tension inherent in games.

In the canned adventures of *Runescape* (as in the built-in quests of *Guild Wars*, too) you can always find out more: you run along to find a pirate or a zombie or a knight or a sorceress, and each time, without fail, they tell you who to see next, what tools you have to find, or where to find a fort. The information is recursive, of course, because it's only telling you what you need to know to take the next step in the game, and because it helpfully refers back to your circumstances immediately previous to where you are now. The game keeps the game going. And when your quest is done, you can always find another.

Even with this wholly artificial and pre-scripted skeleton, however, players find latitude to seek out other players. They build relationships with inworld aquaintances, and even meet real life friends at appointed virtual places and times. This rough and obvious structure of 'the game' or 'the quest' is enough to hang a whole world of legitimate, spontaneous, and surprising social interaction upon. Players chat about how to chop trees, where to bury chicken bones, where to get hammers or medicines – but from there wholly unexpected dimensions erupt from unscripted and free dialogue.

The players make new things happen. They generate new stories. And, thereby, they alter the virtual worlds that host them as *players*.

Non-game worlds (*Second Life, Active Worlds*) have less of a structural need to inform their users of any particular thing – in a way, this makes such a world simply a medium through which other interests or actors may buy, sell, prosetylize, find companions, etc. There is no narrative structure except for those (many) created by the worlds' users.

Second Life

The owners and operators of Club Quake in *Second Life* may create tension, narrative, and drama, by the layout, design, location, and backstory used in making Quake quake. The librarians working on Info Island create a sort of embodied position about the kind of world they would like *Second Life* (and the real world) to be by their choices in design, community building, and offered services. The actors are saying things *in and through* a virtual world, but the world itself has much less to say for itself.

Granted, when you first appear on Welcome Island, you are being communicated with by the Lindens themselves, directly – asynchronously, but directly. The vast and horizonless bluegreen sea says something to you: it's a tame sea, and suggestive of infinite possibilities. The arching white domes and arcing sheets of gray-white walls say something: echoing any number of sci-fi design modes, you may think of this place as an exploded view of the Doctor's TARDIS or the first step toward the at-home version of the *Enterprise*'s holodeck. The step-by-step instructions, offered at an easy pace, say: relax, you're not at work anymore . . . and if you are at work, isn't it time you start treating work as play?

But then the Lindens disappear. You're reminded of them now and again when you wonder about the fluctuating value of virtual currencies, or who builds whatever's at the edge of 'the grid'; but mostly the world's architects shrink as the builders of the world's goods, services, artworks, and social systems (you and a few thousand others) grow large and influential.

Back to initiation

Your expectations about the world are set from early experiences and examples. As one may not expect much from *Worlds.com* (may not expect, that is, to learn much, to see much, to hear much, or to meet many others), one expects a hell of a lot from *World of Warcraft*. In both cases, you learn how much to expect or to what degree you may expect to experience latitude and unexpected possibilities from the initiating moments of the games. *Second Life*'s pale blue holodeck sets a tone of exuberant and elegant fantasy – and the users of the world have gone on to create with wild abandon. We are not disappointed.

The dungeon motif at work in the early moments of *Runescape* (the dungeon serves as a place to tutor new avatars on digging and fighting and talking and moving – the basics of inworld navigation and interaction) lowballs one's expectations of seeing the strange and glorious. That works in *Runescape*'s favor, as the aesthetics of the world are, well, still a bit *blocky*. Lots of cool stuff to see, just all slightly polygonal. You do the early work and are initiated into a world that runs on quests, and those quests are built on the basic skills: slogging in the dungeon.

There is also an element of hand-holding in the game worlds that one doesn't so much sense in the non-game worlds. If I forget who I was going to visit in *Second Life*, I'll just have a miffed friend out there somewhere wondering where the hell I got lost to. In *EVE Online*, I can just check my mission log and get a quick refresher on the next stage of my journey – must go to Planet X and defeat Mining Baron Y. *EVE Online* is actually a good example of a world that works in both ways – there is a structure to fall back on and follow, even as there is liberty to meet folks on your own, devise plans and initiate actions, and generally run amok with glee and unaccountably.

Wherever worlds include games, we find more built-in information resources. Quest or mission logs are available to check, lists of things needed are usually at hand, and canned dialog along the lines of:

> *Lady Belladonna Bids You Welcome! Would You Like to*
>
> *(A) Stay in the Inn?*
> *(B) Learn More About Jousting? or*
> *(C) Return to the Chemist?*

This dialog often easily clickable: you're never far from a tutorial, and never far from getting found if you find yourself lost.

In non-game worlds, avatars must rely on others inworld – folks who have fooled around and figured things out, who know the best places for a new *machinima* dance move, cheetah-pattern hairdos, specialized pornography, or facsimiles of Hermetic texts. Whatever you might be after that is *not* in an official directory is usually best found by *talking with others.*

Some of the official modes of information dissemination to the newbie inworld, however, can help users get started in ways that just talking with others cannot; because other avatars often will not engage in substantive or pragmatic dialog about the world itself, its processes, or its navigation. Most folk inworld want to talk about *builds*, gold, and virtual clothes.

Help from the man

In *Runescape*, after a free account is registered, a character selection screen full of style and color options pops up. You choose a gender (male or female, please), a skin color, then the style and color of hair and clothes. Next is a box explaining the camera controls. Directional/arrow keys pan the camera, and instructions are: find 'Sir Vant'. 'Right-click on him and select "Talk-to" to get started,' it says. If you hang out, just standing motionless for a while, checking out your sporty new hairdo and boots, a big yellow arrow starts flashing on the screen, directing you to read instructions.

Sir Vant is busy with something. He's all duded-up in silver armor, orange shield, sword flashing. You don't get to say anything novel to him: when you click the chat icon, all is pre-scripted. It runs like this: You say 'Hello.' He says, 'Wait a moment, there's a dragon coming!' (That's what the posturing was about.) A big, red, horny, bull dragon charges from the dark side of the dungeon, lets loose a fireball. Vant's squire gets nuked. A goblin drops from the rafters and starts rooting through the remains for valuables. Vant says he could use some help. You're then prompted to click 'continue'.

It's a tutorial. Much more engaging and much more intense than a breezy swagger through a 'Welcome Island', this tutorial sets you up to fight for your survival in the first minute of your time inworld. Vant asks you to take up the goods from amongst the squire's ashes, then dispatch the goblin while he holds off the dragon. Who is Vant? What is the goblin up to? Have Vant & Co. stolen the dragon's treasure or supper or young? Is Vant a villain or a hero? We don't know, we can only act: and with the big red beast stomping and snorting just a few feet away, and with a carbunculous goblin rummaging in Vant's rucksack, there's not much choice apparent. We do as Vant asks; and why? He's holding back the dragon, for one, he hits the visual cues for nobility, for another, and finally – we can't do anything or go anywhere else until we help him. Our allegience is decided by the hard structure of the world: we're with Vant. Now kill the goblin and get on with it.

You move in on the goblin (he's really hitting all the villain notes: plundering, cackling, bent, green), but Vant interrupts you. He shouts something about equipping yourself with the stuff you just picked up off the floor. The game then goes into a tedious but minor script about how to click on stuff and wear it and use it. Once you get the hang of it and you're sheilded and sworded, you click the goblin and hack it up. A green floaty bar turns red above its head as you wreck him. Vant calls you over now about the dragon situation.

Vant has a plan. He's spiked some meat with a mickey, and wants to feed it to the dragon; part 2 of the plan is taking out ceiling support beams. We reckon a woozy dragon is easier to deal with, and maybe the collapse will kill it. The game goads you on again, informing you that you 'have embarked on Unstable Foundations quest' – which is apparently an official 'quest' to kill this dragon. Now for more tutelage. The game yellow-arrows some more icons, showing that the blinking white-and-blue compass rose thing is a 'quest', and telling you how to manage quests. 'Quest journals record what you're supposed to be doing in each quest,' it tells you, and it shows you how to get 'quest help' if you forget what you have to know to do the stuff you're supposed to do (that's on the *Runescape* main site at http://www.Runescape.com/kbase/guid/the_questhelp_system).

The tutorial has you click on the compass icon in the top right of the screen to learn how to orient yourself, then you can walk over to Vant's bag and dig out the meat. Now it's getting to be a bit tedious again – you find a spot in a wall, you're told you can't climb the wall because it's too high, you find a plank to use as a ramp, etc. Finally after planting the meat, luring the dragon, oiling up the wooden pillars, and setting a fuse, you and Vant burn the wood and bring down the ceiling, crushing the drugged dragon.

In this brief how-to session (framed as an adventure, or, more properly, a 'quest') the newbie learns a variety of information sources to consult. The non-player characters, like Sir Vant, tell you most of what you need to know. The tutorial narrator (voicing over the text on screen) tells you the rest. Anything else you might need to know, you can learn through the official quest help screen on *Runescape.com.* And we haven't even yet moved into open play where we can engage other players for information directly. There we move into a world of serious and steady teenage awkwardness that has much more to do with American suburban malaise than it does marlinspike or medieval usury. Yet, somewhat amazingly, *THE Journal* calls *Runescape* 'an online game in which [students] learns about medieval customs and economics' (Starkman, 2007). Anyway, the initiation is complete. *Runescape* gets you started quickly, amping up the game's apparent need for your personal participation – and your need to pay attention and learn basic skills. To move out of the initiation period and into open play, you are essentially *forced* to learn the basics of the world.

EVE Online introduces you to New Eden by having you pick a character from template (you can modify your appearance, make up your own backstory). There are four playable 'races' according to EVE fashion: the Ammarr Empire, the Caldari State, the Gallente Federation, and the Minmatar Republic. The names of the races imply nationality more than race or ethnicity, but there's a lot of loose definition – terms like state, empire, faction, race, ethnicity, and society are used more or less interchangeably in the EVE universe. So when you start mapping out your character, you generate an identity and an avatar based on your selection of political tone, physical characteristics, economic status, and many other factors that work to suggest rough allegiances and one's place within and amongst myriad social groups. For example, the Caldari are a military-industrial state that values technology and security far above arts or liberty; a player who chooses to play Caldari could play it as a straight company-man, or the role might be that of a Caldari far out at the edge of acceptable society. In the course of the play inworld, the character's story may become one of moving closer in toward orthodoxy from unfashionable edge, or it may become one of betraying Caldari values altogether and becoming someone utterly changed.

A word on the background of the world from Wikipedia:

> Set more than 21,000 years in the future, the background story of *EVE Online* explains that humanity, having used up most of Earth's resources, began colonizing the rest of the Milky Way. This expansion led to competition and fighting over available resources. Everything changed with the discovery of a natural wormhole leading to an unexplored galaxy dubbed 'New Eden'. Dozens of colonies were founded and a structure was built to stabilise the wormhole, a giant gateway bearing the name 'EVE'. However, when the natural wormhole collapsed it destroyed the gate. Cut off from Earth and its much-needed supplies, the colonists of New Eden starved. Five colonies managed to return to prominence, each eventually rebuilding their own society. The states based around these colonies make up the major empires in *EVE Online*: the Amarr Empire, the Caldari State, the Gallente Federation, the Minmatar Republic . . .

The world is very well defined, and has a richly imagined history. You just have to join in.

Once an avatar is created (race selected, racial 'faction' choosen, physical characteristics tweaked – beard or moustache, sneer or smile?), the newbie in New Eden has to go through a complex routine of intricate training exercises. There's really a ton to learn – how ships move through space, orbital maneuvers, finding and communicating with other people, finding and trading for goods at space stations, and so on. Lots of bifurcating choices here, too – the kinds of training missions you embark on have repurcussions. Certain skills are built and improved, making you ready for certain kinds of missions; but by choosing one task over another, you may be *less ready* for some missions or situations that will arise in the future. You can't see all ends.

The world itself, New Eden, fits into a *hard science-fiction* genre. The faces are grim, the light is flat and stark, the ships are greasy and creaky and dark. Hard science fiction is typically grimmer than *soft* science fiction, and deals more in technical details of technology. It sticks closely to an agreed-upon physics for the given world. On the other hand, soft science fiction isn't so worried about the technology or the science of the world or setting, as it's typically more focused on the folks in that world, how they feel, what they think, how they love, and what they believe. Although *EVE Online* has a pointed sociological interest (the whole world is structured by the factions and races, and the allegiences and conflicts that follow from these), it is *hard* in terms of the focus on technical detail in gameplay and in its aesthetics. For more on science fiction and its sub-genres, see especially the July 1993 issue of *Science-Fiction Studies* (Vol. 158).

The period of initiation is a period of tedium (if you don't go for the *hard* style), or a time of wonder (if you admire rigorous consistency and fully imagined high-tech worlds). It depends on you. It can be a bit boring to take orders from a fully pre-scripted non-player character for several missions, but the world is so well painted, well designed, and *interesting* that the time flies by. Soon you're out there alone, in the stars, ready for your own adventures. The training period, however, is problematic *as initiation* because, although it educates about New Eden and the machinations of *EVE Online* very thoroughly, it doesn't really ready one for the kinds of common experiences available out there in the rough-and-ready world of mercenaries and miners between the wormholes. The initiation is an initiation into processes rather than stories or symbols – and perhaps that's most appropriate (and most consistent) since we're working within a world of hard science fiction. Process, detail, tool, technology: these, in hard science fiction, are the skeleton on which drama and character hang. In such a light, the highly technical, processual, and *lone*ness of the initiation period may be a very appropriate introduction to this hard, space-faring world.

Symbols of passage

Runescape's initiation clearly offers a 'dangerous passage' (Eliade, 1959) as its main initiatory business. Your new avatar must listen, read, perform, and learn from Sir Vant to best a dangerous goblin and escape from a charging dragon. If you can't beat the dragon and the goblin, you don't get out of the dungeon and you don't gain entry into the world of *Runescape* proper. You have to do it. To not do it is to not live in the new world.

Second Life certainly offers 'bridges' and 'narrow gates' on its Welcome Island. The passage from the various rooms – from 'camera skills' room into the 'communication' tutorial room, on into the flight tutorial – these are connected by a series of short, tight tunnels. And then to leave the Welcome Island tutorials altogether? You must teleport out into the worldmap. Your avatar dissolves into a spiral of pale, smokey spheres – and you are rent from the world. An echo of bodily sacrifice, allowing passage from one world into the next. For in-depth discussion of self-hood in *Second Life*, see Tom Boellstorff's (2010) *Coming of Age in Second Life: An Anthropologist Explores the Virtually Human.*

EVE Online requires the learning of a new language. You leave your old 'way of knowing' behind as you enter into a new world. The lexicon of space travel, mining, and interstellar trade takes root in newbies' heads. If you can't learn the language, you won't be able to go and see and do all that needs to be done in this world.

When you enter a new virtual world, you're entering as something new. Your avatar is not you, but is just some version of you; some aspects magnified, some recessed. The world will bring out attributes, strengths, weaknesses, fears, and virtues that you won't have expected.

This is initiation. Amongst new stars, or out there fending forts from strange dragons in the mud of forgotten swamps, you become someone new. You join a world with a new identity, and you begin to *matter* in a new way.

4

Inworld info desks: information initiation

Abstract: Finding information in online worlds is a primary concern. Without good quality information, games cannot progress, business transactions may fail, and simulations may be incomplete. There are official and non-official (unauthorized) sources of information about virtual worlds. The information about a virtual world may be in the world itself, or in other places online.

Key words: wikis, forums, fans, blogs, newsgroups, directories.

There are two main ways to get information about and within virtual worlds.

One way is that you can get information through official channels, from the world itself (or the worldbuilders). This may be in the form of official Help features, official non-player characters and guides, tutorial features, and so on. The second is by way of all the information that gets generated by users of the world. This comes through the many fan forums, (sometimes extensively encyclopedic) wikis, inworld dialogue, and so on.

The worlds want you to know what you need to know. Every virtual world that makes money from subscriptions has an interest in keeping their subscribers at least informed enough that they don't leave the world due to a sense of frustration with their own ignorance. The more players know, generally, the happier they'll be (which is situated opposite the Real Life adage that 'ignorance is bliss'). Empowered players can make plans, take actions, and try new things. They can develop their characters and contribute to guilds. Information keeps them in the game or in the world.

On the other hand, official outlets can't tell players everything. There are elements of game play that are best discovered, not delivered. Any sense of drama and growth comes from this trial and discovery. There are also things in the game or about the game that players ought not know (a glitch that gives any Orc in your party infinite gold if you stand in a certain waterfall and turn, say, to the left), and though such glitches are tirelessly hunted out and corrected – why advertise them? But unofficial channels – player-to-player communication – are good for just this sort of information. What kind of deals can be designed behind the scenes, off the grid, and carried into the world (and often back out again) for power or wealth?

We'll discuss both of these two main ways to get information; and to begin, here is an overview of the major official and unofficial information channels for our four sample worlds.

Official Stuff

Runescape

Runescape has a 'Game Guide' prominently linked to in the center-top of its main website. Within, we find the Guide subdivided into sections or chapters consisting of:

How do I get started?

Find out how to get started on the road to *Runescape* mastery.

Controls

Learn how to move around the world of *Runescape.*

Combat

Learn about the ancient art of combat in *Runescape.*

Skills

See what skills you can learn in the game.

Quests

View details on all of the Quests in *Runescape*.

Achievement Diary

Explore the world and earn some rewards.

Activities

See what exciting and rewarding activities await you.

Distractions and diversions

Interesting and rewarding regular events.

Random Events

What to do when a random event comes your way.

Miscellaneous guides

View our Game Guides and learn new methods and strategies.

Area guides

Travel the world from the comfort of the Game Guide.

Drilling down, we find further subdivisions. For example, Quests takes you to a page with the following:

Novice Quests

Players new to *Runescape* may find these quests will gain them knowledge through their first steps in the world.

Intermediate Quests

Those who have grown slightly in their experience through the novice stage and seek harsher obstacles.

Experienced Quests

Challengers with enough skill and daring to face the terror of what lies before them.

Master Quests

Quests that only the bravest and most cunning adventurers dare to challenge.

Grandmaster Quests

Quests for the truly bold and heroic!

Special Quests

Massive quests with multiple parts.

Quest listings from A–M

Links to the quests that lie within the Kingdoms of *Runescape*, in alphabetical order.

Quest listings from N–Z

Links to the quests that lie within the Kingdoms of *Runescape*, in alphabetical order.

5 newest Quests

Venture through the new quests that have been discovered in *Runescape*.

Quest experience page

Learn which quests may help you to advance those needed skills.

The QuestHelp system

Customised help, wherever you are in whatever quest.

And, going deeper again by selecting 'Intermediate Quests', we come to a selection of alphabetically arranged articles, each 'article' sharing a title with the quest it describes:

- All Fired Up (Members)
- Animal Magnetism (Members)
- Another Slice of H.A.M. (Members)
- Big Chompy Bird Hunting (Members)
- Cold War (Members)
- Creature of Fenkenstrain (Members)
- Darkness of Hallowvale (Members)
- Death to the Dorgeshuun (Members)
- The Dig Site (Members)
- The Elemental Workshop II (Members)
- The Elemental Workshop III (Members)
- Enlightened Journey (Members)
- The Eyes of Glouphrie (Members)
- The Feud (Members)
- Forgettable Tale of a Drunken Dwarf (Members)
- The Fremennik Trials (Members)
- Garden of Tranquillity (Members)
- Ghosts Ahoy (Members)
- The Giant Dwarf (Members)
- The Golem (Members)
- Hand in the Sand (Members)
- Holy Grail (Members)
- Hunt for Red Raktuber (Members)
- Icthlarin's Little Helper (Members)

- In Aid of the Myreque (Members)
- In Search of the Myreque (Members)
- Kennith's Concerns (Members)
- The Knight's Sword
- The Lost Tribe (Members)
- Making History (Members)
- Meeting History (Members)
- Merlin's Crystal (Members)
- Missing My Mummy (Members)
- Mountain Daughter (Members)
- My Arm's Big Adventure (Members)
- Olaf's Quest (Members)
- Rat Catchers (Members)
- Scorpion Catcher (Members)
- Sea Slug (Members)
- Shades of Mort'ton (Members)
- Shadow of the Storm (Members)
- Slug Menace (Members)
- Smoking Kills (Members)
- Spirit of Summer (Members)
- Spirits of the Elid (Members)
- Tai Bwo Wannai Trio (Members)
- A Tail of Two Cats (Members)
- Tears of Guthix (Members)
- The Tourist Trap (Members)
- Tree Gnome Village (Members)
- Tribal Totem (Members)
- Wanted! (Members)
- Watchtower (Members)
- Waterfall Quest (Members)
- What Lies Below (Members)
- Witch's House (Members)
- Zogre Flesh Eaters (Members)

These intermediate quests (with the exception of one) are available to Members. Members are players who pay dues for bells and whistles like higher-level 'high definition' graphics rendering – and access to special Quests. Next we click on the 'Animal Magnetism' link, and it takes us into a quest description article. Each article has an inworld pic of the quest-in-progress, and a brief overview of the requirements and rewards in the following format:

Introduction

Draynor Manor has a new resident and, adventurers rejoice, she is a damsel in distress! Far from being Sleeping Beauty, she finds the Manor's beds not to her liking and is suffering from insomniac nights. If you fancy yourself able to aid Ava in her search for a good night's sleep, who knows what the budding scientist will produce as a reward?

Quest Information

Members only: Yes
Start point: Draynor Manor
To start: Speak with Ava
Quest length: Short
Minimum Requirements:

- The Restless Ghost
- Ernest the Chicken
- Priest in Peril
- Level 15 Thieving
- Level 18 Slayer
- Level 19 Crafting
- Level 30 Ranged
- Level 35 Woodcutting

There follows some hidden 'spoilers' including the rewards won upon completion of the quest, and a list of the *Jagex* developers who built the quest module.

Higher on the menu tree, and throughout down to the level of individual quest articles, each page has a search feature situated in the bottom-center. Title, descriptions, keywords, categories are available as search modes and limiters, and 'player submissions' can be included in the results.

On the highest-level menu, where we find the Game Guide detailed above, we find the other official source of information – the Help menu. 'Help' subdivides as follows:

Rules of Runescape: Information about our rules and why we have them.
Password support: Information about passwords.
Offence appeals: All about bans, mutes and how to appeal them.
Locked account recovery: Information about recovering your account.
Billing: Find out about our Billing and payment options.
Reporting abuse: Dealing with disruptive players.
Reporting bugs: Information about bugs and how to report them.
Technical: Solutions to your technical problems.
Safety and security guidelines: Advice to keep yourself and your computer safe.
Other: Other information about *Runescape* and *Jagex*.

And each of these categories breaks down into further subdivisions. If you can't menu-browse your way to the information you need, just try that ever-present search feature. *Runescape* does a thorough job of presenting official vectors of information for its users – whether those users are members or just browsers.

Second Life

Second Life presents quite a number of official sources of information; even a quick glance shows that the Lindens use an official blog, Facebook, a YouTube channel, and Twitter. The top-level options on their main site include:

What is *Second Life*?; World Map; Shopping; Buying Land; Community; Help; and Search.

'What Is *Second Life*?' describes the virtual world and what you can expect to do and see in it; it's a pitch for you to join up. 'World Map' gives the current aerial overview for all of the Grid – it's an analog to the satellite imagery composite for the planet Earth in Google Maps. With it, you can get a quick sense of where the hubs of activity, building, and growth are and are not. 'Shopping' offers up information on currency, links to the marketplace, data on current shopping trends, and categories of goods to buy inworld. 'Buying Land' is a big deal in *Second Life*, and information on real-estate trends demands its own upper-level menu. The splash page for Land says: 'In *Second Life*, you can reside in a place that is as unique and special as you are. Live in a friendly neighborhood or buy that private virtual island you've always dreamed of. Perhaps you'll become a landlord, or just host a party for your friends. Here, the weather never puts a damper on your plans.' Subdivisions there include searches for developed land, undeveloped islands or territories, land-use fees, regions, and rental rates and terms. The 'Community' section leads you to that liminal zone between 'official' information about *Second Life*'s regions and the user-generated content that wells up when users get busy creating, well, *community* (but real estate, too, is overwhelmingly user-generated and managed). The 'Help' option will let users submit technical complaints about glitches in the grid, and consult the official Knowledge Base, amongst other options. 'Help' also includes a link out to the unofficial 'community answers' area, where users can ask and answer each other's questions.

A more detailed inspection reveals that these sources are often interconnected – connected to each other through hyperlinks (of course), and connected across media (videos reference blogs, and blogs reference inworld locations, and those islands or buildings may reference maps, and so on). For example, the video that introduces 'Buying Land' called 'Rule Your World' shows a would-be land buyer (a combsome, red-haired white guy in something a lot like a tuxedo jacket) flying over the world map, evaluating islands and neighborhoods. When he finally picks his spot, he melodramatically raises mountains from the sea, all godlike and grandiose, and perches a fully-formed neo-crypto-Ottoman style palace on the highest peak. The video encourages viewers to Buy Land Now (to click the link below the video to buy undeveloped land – so that you too can build mountains and castles), and also to find Events and Groups on the Community pages so that you too can 'Connect with Friends and Meet New People'. The video itself ends with the flourish of lite marriage between the combsome guy and his gothy girlfriend on the highest domed-spire of his new palace. Meeting others and falling in love ('Who Will You Meet?' 'Anything is Possible in *Second Life*.') is a big official push.

It seems that the official modes of communication and information dissemination in *Second Life* are rich, multi-tiered, and hierarchical; yet they are also referential and intertextual, often linking ideas from one area (real estate – Buying Land) to another (meet somebody and fall in love inworld – Community). Bottom menus take residents or visitors to official policy guidelines.

EVE Online

EVE Online has a huge community behind it, and the community (more than the official channels, corporation, or staff) seems to provide the energy that drives the expansion of the game (evidence the live and truly user-generated story of the world, all synchronous across every server, and the fan forums, fiction, art, and community).

Like other online worlds, *EVE Online*'s official channels of information and unofficial channels often overlap and bleed one into the other. The main menu on their website – the extensive left-hand list of headings – carries items that are sometimes both official and unofficial. Links to the Fan Fest, to competition rankings, and to user forums are all condoned and supported officially, but these areas also lack the control that CCP (the Icelandic company that develops and maintains *EVE Online*) can exercise on such things as the Patch Notes, list of Known Issues, or Development Blogs.

Here's the master list of menu options as they stood in the Summer of 2010:

EVE Online

- Screenshots and Art
- Screenshots
- Concept Art
- Wallpapers
- Backstory
- Introduction
- EVE Chronicles
- Short Stories
- Scientific Articles
- Races
- Organizations
- Alliances
- F.A.Q
- What is *EVE Online*?
- Paying for EVE?
- Account Management
- System Requirements
- Customer Support
- The Volunteer Program
- Further Information
- Features
- Overview
- Second Genesis
- New in Castor
- New in Exodus
- New in Cold War
- New in Red Moon Rising
- New in Revelations
- New in Revelations II
- New in Trinity
- Empyrean Age
- Quantum Rise

- Apocrypha
- Dominion
- Tyrannis
- Item Database
- Player Guide
- Purchase Account
- Fanfest
- 2004
- 2005
- 2006
- 2007
- 2008
- 2009
- Community
- Fansites
- Toolkit
- Submit Fansite
- Fansite Toolkit
- RSS Feeds

EVE Forums

- Forum Index
- Dev Finder
- Forum Rules
- Login

EVE Alliance Tournament

- Overview
- Rules
- Format
- Match Rules
- Schedule
- Round 1
- Round 2
- Final Rounds
- Standings
- Round 1
- Round 2
- Forum

EVE Download

- EVE Client
- Tranquility (Live)
- Singularity (Test)
- EVE Patches
- Tranquility (Live)
- Singularity (Test)
- Multiplicity (Test)
- EVE Video
- Gameplay
- Trailers
- The Making of EVE
- 3D Engine Tests
- Community Created
- Fanfest 2008
- Visuals
- EVE Music

EVE Insider

- Player News & Events
- Current News
- Submit News Leads
- Year 105 Overview
- Alliance Tournament
- Archive

- Dev Blog
- Blogs
- Archive
- Patch Notes
- Patch Notes
- In Testing
- Volunteer Program
- Information
- CSM
- Main
- Submission
- Candidates
- Results
- Meeting Minutes
- My Character
- Buddy Program
- Bug Reporting
- Submit Bug Report
- My Bug Reports
- Help

EVE Support

- Knowledge Base
- English
- Deutsch
- Create New Petition
- My Petitions
- Game Policies
- Overview
- EULA
- Terms of Service
- Chat Rules
- Terms of Use
- User Policy
- Reimbursement Policy
- Ban Policy
- Contests
- Known Issues

EVE News

- Game News
- Press
- Press Releases
- Awards and Accolades
- Newsletters
- Quotes
- News Archive

Other items include links to EVE Fanfest, Evelopedia, a Store, Account Managment, and Corporate contact information for CCP. It is an exhaustive amount of information; drilling down into links doesn't as often take you to more subsets of options as is common in other worlds, but hyperlinks to further information in each new page is common. Though the official channels of information are thorough, the corporation doesn't seem to want to overly highlight any strong distinction between the information that it provides and the information that users and players provide for each other. For example, the content in EVE – even the clearly 'official' – is supported by user volunteers who work on many aspects of the game.

A description of the 'Intersteller Services Department' volunteer program:

> There are several branches in the program and each has its own area of interest. These vary from new player support to in game news reporters.
>
> Support Team and Resources (STAR) is the new player support team. They focus their attention on providing assistance to the new players of this world by greeting new players personally and giving advice through both the rookie and normal help channels which players are able to enter and get quick answers to their questions about EVE.
>
> Interstellar Correspondents (IC) are volunteer reporters that together act as the in-game news agency, bringing all of the events, politics and wars from across EVE straight to your browser.
>
> Mercury (M) works closely with CCPs content division to create new fiction and stories thus enriching the fictional background of the EVE universe.
>
> Equipment Certification and Anomaly Investigations Division (ECAID) is the group more commonly referred to as the bug hunters. They work with CCP's QA department to test equipment and features on our test servers before these things are implemented on the live server, Tranquility.
>
> Yulai Archives & Record Repository Team (YARR) are the group of volunteers who help administrate and support the EVElopedia.

Reading the forums, the novellas, browsing the screenshots and artwork – it's very clear that there is something akin to a sense of patriotism widespread amongst *EVE Online*'s core of more serious and committed users. They participate, play, and volunteer because they love the game and love their virtual world. The $15 or so per month that they pay to CCP starts to seem less like a 'bill due' to the corporation as it does a privilege made cheaper by collective cooperation.

Guild Wars

The main horizontal menu at the top of the *Guild Wars* homepage links to Products, Gameplay, Events, Competitive, Community, Support, and a permalink back to Home.

'Products' details the various editions of *Guild Wars* (Factions, Nightfall, Eye of the North, Guild Wars 2), and details the features of each. Factions, for example, features:

- Four new distinct regions to explore.
- Two new professions – Assassin and Ritualist – providing 56 dual-class combinations.
- Three hundred new skills to unlock and use.
- Twenty missions.
- Over 200 quests.
- Alliance battles – large-scale PvP battles that allow factions to redraw the borders of the Canthan empire.

This is part marketing – trying to make a sales point for the potential buyer – and part documentation of factual matters of difference between the various editions of the game.

The 'Gameplay' menu further details these subjects: Game Synopsis; Getting Started; The Professions; Skills; Exploring Your World; Combat; Storage; Costumes; Player vs. Player.

Game Manuals. As we've seen above (with *Runescape*), *Guild Wars* has a large amount of information once we click even two links deep from the major menu subject options. Gameplay to Professions takes us to the following:

Make your choice

Warrior, Elementalist, Monk, Dervish, Ranger, Mesmer, Necromancer, Paragon, Ritualist, or Assassin. Every profession has its own strengths and characteristics, a weapon or magic specialty, and a unique set of skills with which to deal damage, manipulate the enemy or environment, or protect and heal allies. Each profession provides a set of attributes that determines the effectiveness of weapons and skills in battle.

Primary profession

Your primary profession determines your hero's basic appearance, including the type of armor the hero wears. It also provides several attributes that improve skills over time including a primary attribute that is not available when the profession is chosen as a secondary.

Secondary profession

Your secondary profession provides your hero with a second set of attributes and skills to compliment the first. (Your secondary profession does not have access to the primary attribute for that profession.)

The left menu offers links to each of the professions, and each has an introduction to the profession, as well as more detailed points on the professions attributes. The Assassin's page says:

> The Assassin walks the shadows, a deadly viper ready to strike at the heart when an enemy least expects it. Assassins are masters of their chosen weapon, the dagger, and are experts at inflicting Critical Strikes that cause massive damage. The Assassin is trained to efficiently link attacks together in a chain without giving an enemy a chance to hit back. Wearing only lightweight armor, they have mastered the ability to move as shadows, avoiding damage by not being there when an enemy's strike lands. Their other magical skills include Hexes that lower a target's defenses and protect the Assassin from harm.

Assassin attributes

Critical strikes: (Primary) For each point spent on this primary attribute, the Assassin gains an additional 1 percent chance to score a critical hit. Assassins can also gain Energy whenever they score a critical hit in this way.

Dagger mastery: Boost the Dagger Mastery attribute to boost the damage the Assassin inflicts with daggers and the chance to land a critical hit with a dagger. Many skills, especially dagger attack skills, become more effective with increased Dagger Mastery. This attribute also improves your chance of performing a Double Attack and striking with both daggers at once.

Deadly arts: Increase the Deadly Arts attribute to improve the duration and effectiveness of Hexes and other skills that make a single enemy vulnerable to the Assassin's strikes.

Shadow Arts: Put points into the Shadow Arts attribute to improve skills that boost the Assassin's defenses and allow instantaneous shadow movement.

Further official information, contact, and aid comes through the Support options:

Need help with your *Guild Wars*? Check out these resources to find answers.

Support resources

Email support: Request help from the game support team via email

Web support: Use your web browser to request help from the game support team

Guild Wars *Wiki*: Read articles about *Guild Wars* written by other players

Knowledge base: Search the official technical notes to find answers

Account security: Tips to keep your account safe from thefts.

Please do not include passwords in your support ticket or email. You should never give your password to anyone.

Additional resources

Game update notes: Read notes about recent game patches

Network news: Learn the state of the network

Download Guild Wars: Get the *Guild Wars* game client

Download game manual: Download the entire game manual in PDF format

Legal information: Learn more about game policies and rules

Continued bifurcations are plentiful in this support section – Knowledge Base, *Guild Wars* Wiki, takes you to many more subdivisions to help you find information from ArenaNet/NCsoft staff on problem topics often encountered in terms of inworld issues or account matters.

The unofficial stuff

As we've seen in plentiful examples from the above virtual worlds' 'official' channels of communication with their users, the official and unofficial often share and often trespass each other's borders.

By now, a decade into the new century, those who build and run virtual worlds have well-learned the lessons of the Web, so well embodied in the burgeoning of Web 2.0 five years and more ago: let the people do it. Let the users have it. Open the doors, hang out on the porch, share the extra sets of keys. The more open and participatory the model, the longer-lived the endeavor is likely to be. That's fairly well established, and it has become an important factor in the energy and growth of virtual worlds.

Wikis and forums

Wikia.com, the for-profit company started by Wikipedia front man Jimmy Wales and Wikimedia Foundation's Angela Beesley Starling, hosts over 151,000 'wiki communities' with upwards of 2,000,000 user registrations. Its model is built on Wikimedia projects (Wikinews, Wikibooks, Wikimedia Commons, Wikipedia), so its design and use is already familiar to Web users. Wikia encourages the building of wikis that might not stand up to Wikipedia's more stringent standards. That's not a joke. Wikipedia's community demands its entries meet notability standards, be well sourced, that controversies be noted openly, etc. Although built-in social controls exist in Wikia communities too, the users have more latitude to include items that might not meet the standards of Wikipedia. The whole point of Wikia is to foster the growth of wikis about topics that wouldn't make it past the first tier of editors in a general reference source (such as an online enclyclopedia).

Wikia, then, provides a space for what would be considered obscure or inane in general contexts. It's the perfect place for user-generated and user-documented materials on virtual worlds. *Guild Wars, EVE Online, Runescape*, and *Second Life* all have Wikia communities. These, again, are unofficial wikis created by the users of these worlds; they supplement whatever official information may have already been developed – and official channels often include official wikis. *Second Life* and *Runescape* have the most active Wikia communities of our set – 2,330 and 15,691 pages built so far, respectively.

Wikipedia itself is also a great unofficial means of communication about virtual worlds, though the relationship between number of users of a given world, user interest in developing documents about the world, and that world's level of notability for Wikipedia's purposes are all connected. The way it works out in Wikipedia, roughly speaking, is that neurology students write and edit pages about alkaloid receptors, and *World of Warcraft* players write articles about Troll weaponry. *World of Warcraft*-playing neurology students may contribute to both fields. And so on.

The content in forums is also user generated. Folks pose questions, other folks answer and comment. The forums themselves may be hosted by the virtual world (as the EVE Insider is at http://www.eveonline.com/ingameboard.asp) and moderated by forum 'users' who are official staff, or they may spring up in ways and places totally unconnected to officialdom and totally un-condoned and uncommented upon by any agents of the world or its company.

OMG Labs (Otherworld Media Group) hosts a number of *EVE Online*-related services and forums. EVE Search (http://www.eve-search.com/) bills itself as 'Your alternative guide to the *EVE Online* forums', and references plenty of fonts, layouts, and imagery belonging to CCP. Of course, CCP benefits too – the forums are 100% pure *EVE Online* promotion even when they're critical of the world or its policies. No such thing as bad press, as they say.

Alternative forums are plentiful: vBulletin, Neoseeker, and ZAM all host *World of Warcraft* forums. You can go to *Zybez.net* or *Rsboards.com* for unofficial *Runescape* discussions. Ten Ton Hammer is a prime spot for players of *Lord of the Rings Online* to kvetch off the radar.

Forums keep house rules, whether at official world sites or in fan-created domains; but often these are simple. 'No porn, no griefing, don't be a jerk.' Often in the 'benevolent dictatorship' model that most forums and wikis follow, such simple rules are enough. Users 'get it', and if they decide to be a jerk, moderators come out of the woodwork to monitor behaviour, interject themselves into conversations, or eject users outright if necessary.

Fan pages, Blog posts, Newsgroups

Of course, there's more to the Internet than the Web – and there's more to the Web than wikis and forums. Many different types of Web media (and even the new non-Web media of the mobile 'app') serve as unofficial means to talk with other world users about inworld experiences.

EVE Online takes pains on its official site to link to many of the blogs, newsgroups, and forums, and other fan-generated resources that its users have developed (see an impressive list at http://www.eveonline.com/community/fansites.asp).

Want some cheap entertainment? Run a Google image search for wow fan art. Or a Web search for *Runescape* fan fiction.

All kinds of things turn up – totally unvetted, superfluous material. A typical piece of fan art has a purple female elf standing some distance before a white wooded altar. The trees are dark and leafless; it's a cold winter night. Frost lines the forest floor before the clearing for the holy space, and she's standing ready as a warden to defend it. Black hair, black armor, black blade held behind her head. She's ready to swing. But it's winter. And she's just barely wearing any armor at all. Her midriff is exposed, her arms are bare, and her thighs are clothed only in a few straps of leather lacing. Don't get me wrong – the musculature is great.

She's dusky, fit, and she's got 'junk in that trunk' as the Black Eyed Peas would say. But if we're to take this world seriously in terms of its own internal consistency, then we've got some obvious problems. Real warriors would want to armor-up pretty good, right? Throat to ankle? And cold weather would force even the sexiest of elves to insulate, put on layers . . . maybe even wear a hat?

The fan fiction is like that, too. Although pleasant examples exist, the prose is mostly rough and sometimes illogical. It's clear that this end of the user-generated material is used more as a laboratory than as any real boon to the worlds that the works claim to be set in.

But you can find a ton of this stuff, and if you go so far as to make a comment or pay someone a compliment on their buff Orc sketch, then you just might make an inworld ally.

Further discussion

In *Guild Wars*, the information shared with players inworld comes through non-player character contact points. To progress from quest to quest, however minor, you must contact the next non-player lead. All the information needed to complete said quest is available through each new contact, all pre-scripted and pre-plotted. This is the major vector for new information, officially and structurally, though inworld (and in-town) chats with other players provide a wealth of information. Not all of the news and views learned through such chats, however, are helpful or relevant or very interesting – but almost all are revealing. Through chats you learn who is inworld, what tasks they are trying to accomplish, tips on how to accomplish your own, and a glimpse into deeper motivations. (Is this a strategic/mental exercise, a social outlet, is this a way to demonstrate strengths, or to overcome weaknesses . . . a mix and mash of various motivations?)

This two-tiered architecture is universal in virtual worlds.

Official information services are provided by the organization responsible for building and maintaining the world. Unofficial or informal information sources well up from the social play of the worlds' inhabitants.

Worlds.com lets you pick from among several mid-1990s-looking images for your avatar. I went with the penguin for a while. The images, including the bacgrounds, are terribly pixelated. At 'Ground Zero' – the start space inworld – you can usually find other visitors floating around, drifting, trying out movements. There is an information kiosk in the center of the Ground Zero pavilion with information for 'Events', 'Store' and 'News'. Clicking for 'News' caused my browser to open and search for a Windows XP add-on. Finally, the event calendar loaded without an add-on, as a simple Web page (outside of the WorldsPlayer itself). Looks like there'll be some poetry readings next week. I tried to chat with some of the avatars hanging around, but they were all snoozing.

Now I'd like to be able to say that this is not necessarily typical of a *Worlds.com* experience – surely *something* happens here *sometimes* – but after a dozen or so similar experiences with this virtual world, I can say (I have to say) that it is. It's boring. But it's not for its 90s graphics . . . there's something else. Something, despite its *thinness* and *scantness* that I feel it must have in common with even the hippest and hottest virtual worlds. Something I've plainly felt in *World of Warcraft*. Something false; something that *bores*.

And if (in the case of *Worlds.com*) you're there looking to suss out information dynamics, you'll have trouble finding any dynamics at all. The experience initiates one into a near-past view of what the Web could have been. If the Web had evolved from that point forward for the next 15 years, then maybe it would matter and mean something. But it looks stuck in time, obstinate, crass, and rather ugly.

You soon learn that if you want information, you're not likely to get much of it from other avatars, or from the official modes of communication (here I mean the Ground Zero kiosk and the *Worlds.com* website which is also kinda sparse). The calendar of events might be helpful, but even it seems untrustworthy – as of June 2010 there were no dates posted for events (things just roll weekly we presume?), and the site looks like it might have been last updated in, say, 2002. Certainly there was no factual data to make a man think otherwise.

In *Worlds.com* you are brought into a set of dated experiences and taught by a series of object lessons to *not expect to get much information at all* about the world itself, the people in it, their activities, or any future developments. Will there be an update to DMC's world? Will the Reverend Run join him there? Get used to not knowing. A take-away here is that *populated worlds* are *information-rich* worlds. Busy places generate lots of information, and generate novel ways to share and organize the information. Cities have always been engines of cultural innovation, technological ramp-up, and rigorous nodes for information exchange; we may think of well-populated and oft-visited virtual worlds as cities of a sort. The desolate worlds are just hamlets. Just waystations.

But that's *Worlds.com* as something of a negative example. Sir Vant, the Lindens, Ascalon officials, EVE Agents . . . all are there to provide information services to users, and all are provided in an official capacity by their respective organizations or companies.

The unofficial route – which is finding the inworld users who've been around and 'Know Things' – is harder, because it takes a bit of tenacity. How to find those who will actually 'Share what they Know'? And how to find the helpful folks who actually *want* to talk about what they know? None of it is easy for the n00b. It takes a rather delicate balance of tenacity (even *peskiness*) and *cool* (not cool as in 'Man, that's one ice-cold badass motherfucker', but cool in the sense of distant. Slightly disinterested. Detached.). If you're too cool, then you won't elicit any warmth from the good folks who've been knocking around in this virtual world long enough to tell you something useful. If you're too tenacious, then you seem like a nag or a bother, and they teleport to the other side of the galaxy or grid.

Your discovery of, and interaction with, the folks who have some modicum of *salt* inworld is based on a series of what is at first tedious advances. It's not unlike courting a pretty girl. But these 'pretty girls' are probably hairy dudes that live in your cousin's hometown trailer park. Still. You need to know what they know.

Again, user forums, message boards, and wikis are great sources of 'unofficial' information for virtual worlds. Generally, there is more of this fan-generated material for game worlds than for non-game worlds, and that's probably because there's something to *do* in games, and the goals are usually hard to achieve. Tips, tricks, hacks, and cheat codes are necessary for games – but they're not important for non-games (mainly because non-game worlds offer up this stuff freely through official channels themselves). *Second Life* forums are not as common as those for *World of Warcraft*.

Consulting this sort of 'dark gray' literature can be really useful, and can also liven up game play by stoking dialogue in new ways and new dimensions. Even if it's hard to have a conversation in Ascalon, you may find it considerably more easy to get a flame war going on IncGamers.

Forums are interesting for a lot of reasons. Forums (or message boards) are the descendants of the old newsgroups and bulletin board systems (BBS), and the medium just doesn't seem to want to die. Even after Google Groups sprang in to buy up all the old alt-dot-whatever turf, newsgroups continue to be 'sticky' and draw a lot of folks – particularly when there is a need or a want to exchange ideas on a topic near and dear to folks' hearts. Investing hours of the day in virtual worlds? Then there may be a virtual world near and dear enough to your heart to warrant the further investment of time in online forums built around discussing said world and your role in it.

5

Info service inworld: how to practice info services in virtual worlds

Abstract: The practice of research and information service in virtual worlds impacts library services in the Real World. The qualities of libraries in virtual worlds are detailed and the purpose of library services in virtual worlds are critically examined. Some practices for developing and promoting good services in virtual worlds are discussed.

Key words: libraries, virtual libraries, avatars, patrons, branding, marketing.

The way I put it in my previous book (*Building Library 3.0: Creating a Culture of Participation*) is this:

> Virtual worlds are informational worlds; and in the world of information, librarians have an unfair advantage over mere slumlords, pimps, and pushers. Or we ought to. But a survey of *Second Life*, one of the most successful virtual worlds yet, shows librarians to be woefully outnumbered, out-monied, and way, way out-muscled. We are not the victims here – any lack of influence libraries face in virtual worlds is the fault of librarians ourselves. If *Second Life* is good for nothing else, it might be good as a model through which we may consider how library marketing, outreach, and programs work in a very busy, very social, and very sex-and-money oriented world; *Second Life*, like Real Life, is all of these. If libraries can successfully serve communities inside of such a virtual world, we might also learn lessons applicable to growing in our wake-a-day worlds.
>
> (Evans, xx)

I meant it then, and still hold the view now.

Service in these make-believe and half-real (quarter-real? fortieth-real?) places is here taken on its own merits, as an ends rather than as a means; that is necessary for the assumptions I have about the future of virtual service. But I am still very much a physical guy at a physical reference desk (or in a physical classroom) most of the time. The Real World still matters more than any virtual world does, of course. It reads ridiculous to even write such a sentence.

So, as we practice information service in virtual worlds, let us at least remember there is still a Real World waiting for us. Let us try, as much as we may, to take the virtual as a *model* of the real. Once our eyes are bloodshot from staring at low-contrast screens, once our carpel tunnel is inflamed and flaring, once our hands are hungry to handle books again, let's get out there and put whatever we may learn in virtual worlds to work for real people in real life right now.

Deciding to offer inworld information services is a big step, and represents a major change for most information professionals. Private researchers will not have as hard a time shifting as organizations will, since these are usually small companies or single, self-employed individuals who don't have to answer to seething bureaucracy.

This chapter deals with the *how to* of practice in two thrusts: the 'information professional' and 'the librarian'. In this chapter, information professional refers to the private researcher, and *librarian* refers to a librarian working for a public or large private organization (in other words, a librarian in some kind of bureacracy).

Let's talk about librarians first

Librarians famously (or infamously) live in the tension of seeking innovative technology with which to serve their patrons on the one hand, and being stymied by slow moving, change-resistant organizations on the other.

In *Building Library 3.0*, I go into this in some detail in terms of library adoption of mid-oughts social media sites (Facebook, MySpace, etc.) and also talk there at some length about *Second Life*. Though the tone of the conversation in library organizations has become much more relaxed and encouraging about adopting social media (far too lax, actually, in many cases), there still remains some rightful tightwaddedness about investigation of, and experimentation with, virtual worlds.

Public libraries don't have the money or the time, academic libraries (when they have the money and time) often answer to rigid and conservative bureaucrats, and special libraries of all kinds (hybrid systems, military and government libraries, business and law libraries) are way, way too busy with deadline-oriented research to dabble much in the niche communities of virtual worlds unless there is a specific request to do so.

Librarians who want to establish a service in virtual worlds need to: (a) define the kind of service they wish to offer; (b) define the kind of worlds they want to offer it in; and (c) offer firm evidence that the library patrons who matter – which is to say the library patrons who spend money, organize events, and know political bigwigs, have opinions about policies and make them known (as opposed to patrons who don't care or don't think we care whether or not they care) – are already established in said virtual worlds.

Lots of exuberant librarians just feel eager to get in on virtual worlds – to build machinima, avatars, and islands inworld – without thinking through the *why* of their proposed *service*. It's that word *service* that is of primary importance. If the reason for building inworld is *not* to serve your patrons, then the librarians' time spent in virtual worlds is wasted, and maybe worse: if your aim is not to serve, then you're just wasting the taxpayer's money on a toy.

If the need is real, if patrons are inworld and could use help navigating and finding information, then the librarians are needed inworld too.

With evidence of patrons using virtual worlds (building an .mp3 store in a virtual mall on an island built by The Electric Sheep Company, for example), librarians have a legitimate entry into virtual service. The key here is to go back to your Real Life interactions with patrons – Who in your community has a garage band? Who blogs about online dating? Who has the serious gaming addicti – er, interest? You find out who your patrons are, what they are interested in, and how they are using virtual worlds to promote themselves. Learn their inworld handles, their favorite gathering spots, which worlds they like and why. Ask if you can join them sometime – see where it leads.

Once you are welcomed into a virtual community, you'll need to set up shop in a more serious and semi-permanent way.

The most baroque and grandiose example of how to do this has to be Alliance Library System's *Second Life* Library project (also called Info Island or Community Virtual Library). Now seven years old (and now renamed a number of times – from Info Island, to Information Archipelago, to Community Virtual Library), the project has been very steady and persistent in efforts to grow its presence inworld. It's done really good work too, and has received buzz and press outside of traditional librarian-to-librarian chatter.

The core of the project is simple – an analogous library 'building' with plenty of reading room, hang-out space, bookish decoration, and working OPACs. And, most important, a well-staffed reference desk. Interested librarians with access to *Second Life* from anywhere in the world may volunteer to staff the library, but in actual practice the librarians tend to be from the urban United States. Avatars wandering into the place will find that librarians often initiate contact – asking if and how they can help you find information.

Elsewhere I have criticized *Second Life* Library and similar initiatives for putting non-patrons first. I made a somewhat shouty case that serving random, meandering avatars in a virtual world before the locals is not just a bad idea, but was in fact unethical. If local land tax dollars keeps your operation afloat, and you keep a local resident waiting for service – even if just for an instant – you are abusing the trust of the taxpayers. This still stands as true, though there is plenty of room to move leeward of this general position in cases of exceptional need. It could be the case, for instance, that your local patrons want to see a virtual library presence developed to draw attention to the town. Or they could see setting up a virtual library inworld as a way to connect with a sister city.

Generally, though, the point remains solid: serve locals first. This is a tough maxim to live by when you're inworld, greeting any old avatar who happens to fly by. It's also a tough one to stick to at large inworld author events, like virtual book talks, or lectures on the virtual library campus given by some invited luminary or other. When you are inworld, your attention is inworld.

It seems clear, then, that virtual library service and realtime Real Life reference desk service does not mix well. A passage from my previous book (ibid.) on the tensions between virtual and real, between moneyed and poor, is again relevant:

> Zygmunt Bauman got some deserved buzz in the late 1990s for his take on globalization, and it deserves some play here, in terms of libraries. Bauman . . . put his take on the tensions between global and local forces in terms of commerce, travel, communication, and other dimensions. He threw new light on the means of the powerful to move through space on their own terms. Partly framed as a study of disparity between 'globals and locals', his view of the 'local' person was of one who was stuck spatially, having to settle for the circumstances of places he couldn't leave – but also having the luxury of time to explore said place and live in it fully. This quantity

> of time, though enforced by an inability to escape the bounded space, was time that a global person lacked. On the other hand, though he may have little or no time to enjoy it, the global is so free of place and the physicality of space, which he may enter a sort of 'cyberspatial heaven' in which bodies don't even really matter anymore.
>
> Bauman's views on globalization are relevant here – it is the 'global person' who may enjoy virtual realms like *Second Life*. Even if a patron is very locally-bound, and comes into the library to enjoy the free computer lab, it is only thanks to a global system of infrastructure built thanks to great riches provided by the labor of locals all over the world that she can do so at all. Well, when does she stop being local and begin being a global? When does the yam farmer on his mobile phone, outside of Shongolo, Mississippi, become a global? I think this question of distinction matters, though it is not a question I can answer here.
>
> There are, no doubt, many benefits to serving a global community for both those served and for the library doing the serving. Many of our services here in the late ought-oughts are already global and do already reach non-local patrons. Virtual reference service through e-mail, instant messaging, phone texting (or for that matter, contact through *Second Life*), often make no differentiation between patrons who e-mail from down the road or from across international shipping lanes. Good librarians give it their best each and every time, and that is as it should be; just as we don't ask for proof of citizenship upon admitting entrance into our stacks, we should not *in principle* turn queriers away because they cannot provide proof of locality.
>
> (2009, xx)

But then we're not always on the reference desk, are we? As long as you (individually and collectively as an organization) have your priorities straight, you can begin working on the service you'll offer inworld without any sense of mixed priorities, betrayal, or guilt. But keep revisiting the issue of when, where, and how the virtual may be stepping on the toes of the Real. Real should always be given priority. Repeat: the Real World and your real patrons should always come first.

What'd I just say? Who comes first?!

Alright.

So we can learn some things from *Second Life* Library.

Inworld library attributes

It is an 'open' kind of thing; under the Procedures link on the Community Virtual Library's main website, instructions are posted for adding items to the community calendar, getting permissions, and organizing events. You don't have to have been a part of the club to get involved – and, by getting involved, you become part of the club. Anyone with a good idea and the skills and determination to make the idea bear fruit can get in on the action. In fact, to grow the project the library needs more participants, volunteers, and organizers.

It's an experimental thing. The whole operation started as an experiment, and the history of this library has been a history of trying to make new ideas work, re-working bad ideas, learning from mistakes, and re-tooling for the future. Silliness sometimes comes through rather than quality content (their 18th May 2010 blog post comes to mind: 'If you haven't visited the Exercise & Fitness area on Info Island, why don't you join us for a 20 min work out session next week? Monday, May 24; Wednesday, May 26; and Friday, May 28 at 7 AM SLT we'll meet to get moving! The area has several animations for exercise and dancing, so put your AV to work while you work out in real life.'), but what the hell? At least they try new programs.

It's a well-organized thing. Just take a look at the Virtual Reference Desk calendar – the shifts (usually over 12 hours a day) are booked for today, tomorrow, next week, next month, and *years* into the future. Now things change, and the people who volunteer this month may not be able to next year, but there is enough interest and enough built-in organization to fill the slots with whoever is able to volunteer for the foreseeable future. Looking at the events calendar, there are constant training events for these virtual librarians, inworld community outreach, book groups, and author visits. They're not just shooting from the hip, this bunch. They're organizing for the future.

But *Second Life* Library is not a perfect thing, and, as I mentioned, there is plenty of points of criticism to be made. I'll elaborate on some of those now, but none of this is meant in a mean spirit: as an effort at inworld information service, *Second Life* Library does a lot right. But what can they do *better*?

The three biggest concerns have to do with the 'echo chamber' effect, sharing valuable skills with patrons, and establishing or defining a community of patrons.

'Nextgen' librarians have created a culture that reminds me of Jaron Lanier's 'digital Maoism' in that certain ideas and principles having to do with community collaboration have become sacred cows. Some of these ideas are good, some are not adequately tested, and some are just plain bad. For example, an 'open' OPAC that allows tagging and patron comments is a good idea. The idea (and actual effects) of libraries using social networking sites to connect with patrons has not yet proven its worth or longevity. And using local tax dollars to serve global comers inworld is probably a bad idea.

But the perceived 'sacredness' of NextGen values leads quickly and clearly to an echo chamber in which each NextGen librarian more or less sounds like every other NextGen librarian. That, in turn, makes it difficult to levy criticism without sounding like a Luddite. In the Spring of 2010 I gave a talk to a wide array of librarians through a Learning Times and Alliance Library System web conference (Innovation for Libraries in the 21st Century, it was called). My talk was titled 'Why Librarians Should Stay the Hell Away from Facebook.' Reading the blogs and tweets after the event, I wasn't surprised to see a criticism of 'elitism' tossed my way. My perspective in the talk was essentially a stance against Facebook as a pro-working man argument; that is, getting our heads out of our twitter accounts and back to developing initiatives that really help those in need. Being called elitist left me with the distinct impression that to even raise the prospect that 'a social networking tool' was not universally necessary and good was out of bounds for NextGen thinkers. I've also taken heat for my ambivalent attitude toward virtual worlds in the past (which is one reason I wrote the present text: things are usually more complicated than they at first appear).

This NextGen brand of digital Maoism is in danger of creating a bunch of nodding yes-men, and of creating a standard of 'participation' whereby everyone jumps on the newest social media tool without honest criticism and discernment. Is NextGen over yet, for goodness sake?

Now don't get me wrong – you've got to try things and experiment before you can discern. So I do not argue that librarians should stay away from innovative tools or social networking or virtual worlds or anything else. Only that librarians, stewards of expensive public resources that they are, must not be afraid to think critically about these new tools to see how (or if) they can be put to best use for the patrons that we serve.

Second Life stands out as a major example of how librarians got on board (hard, fast, early) without discerning their purposes inworld. There is a very simple question that I continue to ask: what good does *Second Life* Library do for the patron who walks up to my reference desk tonight? The question continues to stump good-hearted librarian-cosplayers.

But it is a serious question, and a question looming over this entire book. It works on the assumption that your organization is serving patrons inworld, or creating new communities of patrons to serve within virtual worlds; this is a look at what all that means, of how to serve, of what happens in these virtual worlds when we go in as information professionals and librarians. This question of how it helps the patron at my reference desk tonight, however, is going to have to be worked out by any serious organization making forays inworld and by every individual who wants to serve there. It simply is not enough to create an avatar and ghost around your virtual campus.

So what good does *Second Life* Library really do for the patron who walks up to your reference desk tonight? It will take more than NextGen group-think to sort that one out.

Real skills for real patrons?

Another ongoing issue with *Second Life* Library is what content or services they provide to their patrons. And, the word *patron* only loosely applies here – no one is actually offering *Second Life* Library patronage except for the taxpayers in the Alliance System (Illinois). In the loose sense of patronage, lots of avatars do wander through the library's Information Archipelago. In fact, the patrons of Alliance (and the 'patrons') of *Second Life* Library, are paying Linden Lab (Linden Research, Inc.) for the right to maintain a presence and services in *Second Life*.

We should wonder what benefit these patrons get for their time there. A library is a place to learn skills (research skills, special skills through community programs and the like) – but what evidence of quality service and education do we find for *Second Life* Library?

Actually, here they do quite well in some ways. Given that their patrons are inhabitants of a virtual world, the skills and programs available are rather appropriate to the environment and social milieu. So music events, a Shakespearean actors club, storytelling, and *joust* practice (yes, riding forth and knocking your opponent with a pole – jousting) probably hit a sweet spot for the *Second Life* Library community. Beyond formal programming (the list above being sampled from the July 2010 calendar), plenty of opportunities exist to learn skills from other patrons and from the library staff through casual interaction.

A stroll around the Archipelago offers up the chance to chat with wanderers and regulars. We meet random stray teleporters as well as those who came to find the library. If you need to improve your machinima dance moves, your prim's Havok elasticity, or your inworld brand buzz, try just striking up a conversation with folks. Somebody you meet in the Archipelago – or for that matter, anywhere inworld – may have what you need. Sadly, some of the most basic precepts of information literacy are pretty far from mundane or commonplace.

The concept of orderly naming conventions for personal notes, books, objects, and devices is apparently alien enough to the average 'advanced content creator' in *Second Life* that one of the official guidebooks finds it necessary to give a basic lesson in record/object findability. In the 'Giving Descriptive Names' section of the introductory chapter, we read:

> Rather than naming your new pair of jeans My Pants, why not make it something more unique, like Blue Jeans with Red Heart Pocket Detail? You don't have to be that specific, but doing so lets you and any poetential customers search for things like *blue jeans*, *jeans*, *heart*, or *pocket* and find it quickly. By naming Inventory items as accurately as possible, you can make it easier to find what you're looking for.

It goes on:

> There's no reason not to put keywords in an Inventory item's name if it makes it easier to find . . . you don't have to be overly descriptive; it's just something to think about. There's nothing stopping you from naming your pants Outfit 4 – Pants, but that can get pretty confusing for both your customers and yourself!

And finally:

> A little descriptive naming makes your Inventory far easier to search.
> (Weber *et al.*, 2008: 13)

That last line is a fairly efficient summary of the totality of the coursework needed for a master's degree in library and information science. Don't you wish you'd just bought the guide to *Second Life* instead of taking out student loans, now?

This is a rare glimpse past *glam* into a real issue about real *technique*. You actually don't learn technique like that in graduate school – you learn at the reference desk, or by sweating out metadata for weird records or *realia*. Technique can't be taught so much as it has to be learned. So, I reckon, we cannot really blame the librarians at home in *Second Life* for not addressing matters of technique, and for leaving the discovery of its importance to chance and guide books.

Actually, this all stands as a great opportunity. How many patron-accessible and keyword-searchable databases exist for Universally Unique Identifiers (UUIDs)? How many inworld 'biblographic instruction sessions' (let's get a new term for that, please) teach UUID syntax? Any working groups set to roll out a bridge between Library of Congress Classification and UUIDs?

But wait. These librarians are professionals, and they do help with complex search tasks (tasks for which an understanding of information techniques such as the one above are integral and integrated). These are degreed professionals who serve in Real Life libraries, volunteering to serve inworld. They know databases, Web search, and e-books, and so are able to teach advanced research skills and search syntax, which enables patrons or visitors to go further on their own whenever they need to. Patrons may not know *what* or *how* to ask.

It may take the frank engagement of other information professionals (pros who aren't so wowed by the glow of virtual skies) to point out that the basics have to be established for our patrons' info literacy skills inworld just the same as they do in Real Life.

Who is the community? Who are the patrons?

Here in the early part of the new century, the matter of 'who' your patrons are and 'where' they live is not yet much of a sticking point. But as distance gets *dead*er, as Cairncross might say, these issues will become more important and more testily contested.

Second Life Library has a wide-open door policy. If you can clear the hurdle of joining *Second Life* at all (membership is free, but the cost of access is not), then you may have access to the *Second Life* Library's services. It's a standard library model – anyone may enter, anyone may make use of the resources; but the standard library model for Real Life may not be sustainable inworld.

The old question remains: why should we locals pay for online reference services for you globals? As economies swell and sag, as environmental and geopolitical changes force migration, and as regions all over the world work to re-assess value in the fallout of the Great Recession, it's a question that may increasingly catch in our collective throats.

Even if one is gracious enough to side with arguments for radically open access for other reasons (won't it make the world a better place . . . everybody deserves a chance to learn . . . or even why should I care what the hell my local librarian does when she's not shelving books?), the brass-tacks of economics will still eventually come calling. If things get really hard, your library may be on the county comptroller's chopping block. If your librarians are flirting with *Second Life* glitteratti rather than getting up and showing patrons how the stacks are organized, your case will not be helped. The comptroller is just looking for a reason to lay off staff – and he'll close the doors to the library altogether, if he has to.

Well. You see where I'm going with this. *Second Life* Library 'service' to their 'patrons' remains full of interesting problems.

Where to lurk

Any discussion of where and why to offer information service inworld has to be informed by a good foundation in knowledge of who uses which worlds, and why they use it. This is closely related to some of the issues that arise when libraries 'offer' social networking services to patrons – specifically, it gets to the 'look who's in the food court' issue. If you're at the mall, hanging out and having a good time looking for hotties, you don't want to glance up and see your librarian offering you a pamphlet on Boolean Logic. So do patrons really want to 'friend' their librarian (or their cardiologist, or their mayor, or their accountant . . .) on Facebook? And do patrons really want to 'hang out' with the librarian when they're hunting Orc in Azeroth?

Where, then, are information professionals needed, or where could information professionals be useful? Of all the virtual worlds we've talked about (and of the many others that we haven't), which are best suited for information services?

To establish criteria for deciding where to serve, again look at the patrons. If folks are inworld to play a game just to *have fun*, a librarian won't usually be necessary.

If folks are inworld to *make money* (whether in a game or a non-game world), then they could use information services. If folks are inworld for political reasons (to garner support for issues, etc.), then they could use information services (whether they know it or not). If folks are inworld to spread information (or raise awareness, or however it may be fashioned – and this is closely related to politics), then they could use information services. And if folks are inworld for educational reasons (to teach, to learn, to research), then they could use information services.

Which are the worlds in which people are looking to make money, do politics, be an activist, or do research?

Second Life has to be the first on the list. People spend time there to make money, to campaign for issues, and to hold classrooms – so *Second Life* meets all of our criteria for a world in which to offer information services. The early history of *Second Life* is mainly a history of economic hype. It was going to be *the* virtual world – *the* new way to do online commerce. Later it found a groove as an alternative space for distance education, and it seems to be holding to that identity fairly well.

In any case, *Second Life* still seems to be the world of choice to offer information services. It's the biggest world with the most serious inhabitants (and by 'serious' I mean *interested in money, politics, or education*). However, your 'choice' may not matter much. You have to work in the worlds your clients use, or create a base in a new world.

Surely researchers slog through *Runescape*, *World of Warcraft*, and other worlds – plenty of evidence exists in the literature, plenty of successful virtual ethnographies await you in databases. And the work is still being done, from the roving journalism of James Au, to the serious sociology of nethnographers, to something somewhere in between, the field is rich and busy; it's not hard to find researchers in any given virtual world. Some worlds lend themselves to research more than others, though, at least insomuch as that it's hard to *do* research if your avatar is under threat of *salamander talisman bastard sword*. The likelier you are to get picked out of the crowd and beaten, the harder it may be to pose questions and find answers (unless it's the case that you're looking into some aspect of random virtual ass kicking for a patron or client – fair enough).

Viral you

You (as an individual information professional or as an organization) need to brand yourself inworld. If it is information services you offer – research services, data aggregation, surreptitious investigation – then 'information' or 'research' or 'investigation' should be the first thing potential clients or patrons see. Put it in your avatar's name: P.I. Smith or Researcher Suzy Q. The immediate connection between your services and the clients' needs must be highlighted whenever possible.

Some of this can be done casually. By dropping in and hanging out in *Guild War*'s Ascalon City or on the Welcome Island in *Second Life*, for example, you're able to chat with other avatars. The more you chat, the more likely it will be for you to share who you are and what you do. As you learn a bit about the person you're chatting with, you can present your skills in such a way that addresses his or her specific needs and concerns. This is a slow process, and it may take a long time before you meet someone with whom you can actually do some business. You'll get a lot more grief than you will get leads for work.

Another informal way to promote yourself is to announce your services and skills to a whole room or world. Different worlds allow for different ways of doing this. In *Guild Wars* the default chat mode is public – a sort of always-on chat room. Such a chat room would be the kind of venue you'd look for to make a casual shout-out to yourself: Research w/15 yrs experience – anyone looking to find something? This tactic hits a lot of people all at once, which can be good, but any single message is more likely to get drowned out in the chatter. So be prepared to repeat (and repeat) your pitch . . . while somehow not coming across as desperate or as a griefer yourself. You'll also want to check the Terms of Service of the world you're in – does it forbid this sort of advertisement (see Appendix II)?

Self-promotion may also be done formally and with a more carefully considered purpose.

In *Second Life* it may be worth your time and money to build an island or to buy land. Like real estate in Real Life, land values change (that's about where the similarities between *Second Life* and Real Life end). In fact, value may be affected by how quickly things change inworld. In some ways we might expect land value to be meaningless – after all, you're always neither near nor far from any other place in the entirety of the virtual world. You can teleport anywhere you want to go – so living 'close' to your favorite mall doesn't really matter at all. But on the other hand, regions and neighborhoods do have tones and attitudes. If your neighbors are building things you'd rather not see, or saying things to you that you find offensive, you won't want to live in the neighborhood for long. And this principle still exists in *Second Life*; no matter how often or how far you teleport, you want home to be wonderful when you return to it. As a promotional video for virtual land says, you're not just buying property – you're buying into a neighborhood, a hangout spot, a social space. Making sure you like the people close to your spot may be worth paying for.

Shopping for land in *Second Life* is kind of fun. When you start browsing options, you'll notice a tree of choices – Developed or undeveloped? Thematic regions, or scripted Linden Homes? If undeveloped – what sort of island, or what sort of land? If open (non-island) land, how much are you willing to bid for it?

Creation of online (but not inworld) outposts may help shore up your efforts at marketing services inworld. Using more traditional tools, like blogs and wikis, can help establish you to inworld markets, as info seekers search for the services of information professionals. If your strength is finding values and buyers for old comic books and trading cards, developing a wiki on the subject as a testament to your interest and expertise can make you a notable name amongst inworld traders even when you're offline and in the hot tub.

Designing an inworld presence (whether or not it has any inworld property) is a complex and multi-faceted endeavor. Books about inworld marketing campaigns are plentiful, and Linden Labs has a number of 'official guides' (published through Sybex) to developing land, writing machinima scripts, fine-tuning your avatar's appearance, and making money; there's no lack of information on how to set yourself up formally and properly as an official organizational entity inworld.

Both the informal methods and the more assertive styles of presenting yourself, or your organization and the skills you bring to bear, must consistently come together in your interactions with other avatars. There's a fine line here. It's easy to turn people off when you're always on self-marketing mode. Remember Bob Vance, from *The Office*?

> *Phyllis* [at the Christmas party]: Hi, guys. Does everyone know my boyfriend, Bob Vance?
> *Kevin* [introducing himself to Bob]: Kevin Malone.
> *Bob Vance*: Bob Vance. Vance Refrigeration.
> *Stanley*: Stanley Hudson.
> *Bob Vance*: Bob Vance. Vance Refrigeration.
> *Ryan Howard*: Ryan Howard.
> *Bob Vance*: Bob Vance. Vance Refrigeration.
> *Ryan Howard* [Kevin, Stanley, and Ryan all smile to themselves]: What line of work are you in, Bob?
>
> (IMDB, 2010)

But if you never tie your skills to your avatar, nobody will know to go to you for the research help they need, just as the guys from Dunder-Mifflin mightn't have known to go to Bob for a new mini-fridge. Informally and formally, officially and *on the sly*, you have to promote your organization's services and your information brokering skills with care and with purpose and with vision. That's not easy.

And through all this, you may find yourself taking *Second Life* or your *World of Warcraft* guild very seriously. This is a common affliction for people who spend time inworld, if it is an affliction. What you begin to notice is that people do take it very seriously – they do 'live it', as it were, even though it's just a simulation. All this implies that maybe it's not *just* a simulation. Maybe the simulation becomes yet another forum for real experiences, and for real personal meaning.

It's beyond our scope to dig deeply into the psychology of the inhabitants of virtual worlds; it's just enough here for us to say that we must take them (and their worlds) seriously and on their own terms. We assume a certain amount of 'reality' to do business with them in an equitable way. They live, at least some of the time, in a virtual world, and so shall we too.

But, all that said, the straight-faced-ness of it all can strike a guy funny. Just don't laugh aloud.

Linden, Turing, and Kempelen's Turk

Our 'virtual ontology' hasn't substantially moved much beyond the clockwork ontology (in turn, a heavily physical and Newtonian ontology) of 1769.

The Lindens and NCsoft let us use a kind of sleight of hand on each other; millions of virtual worlds participants twirl and giggle and make hard-nosed deals with each other. The net effect is that it looks like our play/pretend (or our virtual) worlds are actively teeming with digital, interconnected, and machine-driven intelligences. We have trouble telling who is player and who is non-player. We have trouble distinguishing between human others in disguise and non-human others running scripts.

The famous test Alan Turing proposed for detecting machine intelligence gets turned on its head here. It's not that we are looking for machines suitably intelligent that they might fool us into thinking that they are human. Variations on this idea become more interesting; we are on the look out (in *EVE Online* and *Second Life*, especially) for groups of humans who can display adequate intelligence to suggest to us that they might be a function of the world itself – a pre-programmed flock of avatars just crunching code. Which organizations, which buildings, which relics and business ventures are auto-generated, and which have a real life bad-hair-day human being behind it all?

We've gone well past the days of the Turk of Kempelen (so wonderfully chronicled in Tom Standage's 2002 book), when some of us wanted to believe that a pattern of mechanical configurations and a pattern of ideas overlaid on the physical machinery could be invested (or vested) with intelligence or something more. We are beginning to edge on past the concerns of Turing, too, as we can now see that 'sounding human' is getting easier to do.

In virtual worlds, we are in a constant blind. We don't know which actors are human or are non-human. Most of the time we may be able to cipher a player from an NPC – but so often, too, real humans are behind the strangest and most bizarre behaviors. We encounter actors that we assume to be humans-behind-avatars participating in autismal activities that are not clearly non-machine generated. It is in this environment of ambiguity – one in which machines haven't so much risen to the level of disguising themselves as potentially human, but instead one in which humans have found themselves often akin in action to the obsessive fixations and compulsive repetitions of machines – it is in such worlds that we plod forward, always vying to connect with another. Always looking for a hand to touch, and hoping that that hand, whether or not it is under 'intelligent' control, is at least *human-like* enough to offer some warmth and comfort.

Virtual worlds, like Real Life, can be lonesome and cold. Information professionals from all camps would do well to remember that loneliness is a primary motivator for many of our patrons and clients.

Part II
Time Inworld

The first part of this book looked at information services and information-seeking behavior in virtual worlds; in the second part, I want to share play-by-play experiences of actually spending time in virtual worlds, and then suggest ways that the worlds will molt into something new. The following does not even pretend to approach a formal ethnography of virtual culture, but (such as it is) is explicitly concerned with moving through virtual worlds as an information professional.

Simply put, here are my experiences as I spend some shoe-leather trying to reach out to other actors in various virtual worlds. My interactions are by and large concerned with getting and sharing information. I've shared accounts of 'initiations' into virtual worlds above; the episodes below take off after the initiation into *Second Life*, on which I concentrate, is complete.

The final chapter and the conclusion move us past the particulars of the current palette of virtual worlds, and into a discussion of what might come next. Virtual worlds as we know them now have a limited life span. When they fail and fade, information professionals must be ready for the post-virtual: augmented reality. With the convergence of the burgeoning physical (tactile, gestural, and neural) interfaces and the ubiquity of personal mobile information devices, the folding of 'virtual' spaces into natural spaces is set to suck all the oxygen out of the room. If there are any lessons to be learned from the likes of *Second Life*, now is the time to learn them. A world of amphibious patrons living in an in-between world of digital shadows and physical artifacts will shortly demand all of our attention.

6

Hungry Ghosts in *Second Life*

Abstract: Many libraries in Second Life are empty and unattended. These libraries appear deserted, and visitors may be confused as to their purpose. Librarians should find better ways to spend their energies than the development of such empty virtual spaces.

Key words: academic libraries, public libraries, public library policy, tax payers, promotion of library services.

I was hanging out in a main waystation for newcomers (Waterhead Welcome Area) and decided to try a cold pitch to a room of random strangers. 'Hi,' I said, 'I'm a professional researcher. Anybody need help finding some info?' No responses. Nothing. I walked to the gaming table by the north rail, and looked out at the sea. Always the same – perfectly periwinkle, perfectly calm. The game was on a chessboard, but the pieces were bubbly orange and white. Dreamcicle colors; who knows what game.

I tried my pitch twice more, chatting to the open room. Pavilion, really. On the third try (which was to be my final for the night), I got a hit. Monday (we'll call him) piped up: 'What's memes[?]'. At first I wasn't sure the message was for me; there were other conversations going on. Some folks were talking about the Linden's optional credit card info taken upon registration. Then he said: 'Saw the site. What's memes?'

He'd looked at my *Second Life* profile and clicked through to my personal website. I had a post up about a collaborative book project called *The Future We Deserve* and wrote a brief response to Thomas Bjelkeman-Pettersson's essay 'Memes That Kill'. Monday was curious.

'Memes,' I said, 'Are ideas that spread like viruses.' This was my best lead yet, and I thought it might lead to more information exchange, maybe even a minor gig. But nothing. Monday had lost interest and wandered back over toward some well-dressed newcomers.

To the north-west, a strange scene was developing. A dinosaur was moving in from behind a public fountain; it was dinosaur-like, anyway. Mostly in blades and sheets of blue and black, it stalked up toward the pavilion, then seemed to phase through it on its way to the sea, all the while chatting lightly with onlookers.

It barely caused a stir.

Deep and dark

I searched the world map for libraries. I saw my usual spots around Info Archipelago, but was surprised to see a great many more than when I'd last visited. Cybrary City II caught my eye. I teleported in to see a low brick wall with yellow signs advertising lots of different kinds of spaces, mainly educational and cultural stuff.

The description for Lilith's Library of Myth, Mysticism, and Magic, one of the spaces in the Cybrary City region, reads: 'From ancient ruins comes the knowledge of Gods, mystical creatures and magical existence. Come dig through this library and experi[e]nce life told by those who were there first-hand.' I touched the sign, and teleported in.

You start on a wide portico of muted colors. A gray obelisk set with the Elder Futhark runes Wunjo, Laguz, Sowelo, and Jera (forgive my rough transliteration) on each of its four sides, is slightly to the right, and two rust-colored columns rise to either side of you. You've teleported in onto a bright blue-green pentagram in a black circle. You soon realize that you're under water – the whole building is sunken, flooded.

The runes, if I remember my Ralph Blum rightly, stand for joy, flowing water, the Sun, and changing seasons. I guess that must mean something. Water we got, though flowing it's not. The sun is up there somewhere, but there's little light down here. Joy? OK, we can feel joy. Why not. And changing seasons.

There are white and red-brown marble columns with turquoise tile-work on the bases. These are Corinthian; they do give the place a certain sense of venerability – like this sunken place might have been here in Atlantean times, and Lilith has only just happened upon it here in *Second Life* by accident somehow.

Turning to the south, there's a wide, dim hall with a low brown desk in the corner, and pictures hanging on the walls. One's got a beast embracing a naked lady – a click reveals it's meant to be Lucifer with a lover or a victim. Other pictures sit level on the mossy walls, and after a while I wonder what kind of a library this really is. How is it that this can be called a *library*? There are no books, no scrolls, no newspapers – just the images on the walls; but then this all presents a bigger question: in a virtual world, there are no physical objects (no books, no papers), and so we must wonder if any object could become 'a book' in the sense that it is an icon presenting access into a great deal of text (or video, audio, or other types of information)? The answer is: absolutely, yes. What makes this strange, sunken, museum-like place a library? In as much as it collects, organizes, and provides access to information, it is a library of a kind.

We are having to liberalize our definitions, though, to accommodate the assertions of Lilith's Library. We could broaden our definition wide enough to say that the whole damn world is a library if we wanted, and the term 'library' would then be meaningless. But there may be more of a case for calling an entire virtual world a library than for saying the same of Real Life. We'll leave the use of this, now, to your own speculations.

Official signage

Back up top, in the open air. I teleport around a bit and find Kansas State Library's virtual branch. On the campus, there's a Historical Museum, and outside of the little wooden schoolhouse façade, there's a campsite set up. Slightly farb, but interesting. A big digital painting to commemorate Buffalo Soldiers, several canvas tents, campfires, a kettle of something bubbling over the coals. On the far end of the site, there's a sort of tin horse. I sit on it and have a good look around.

This is a perfectly *built* place, as opposed to a place that imperfectly grows, changes, evolves; from the boxed-out samples of Kansas geological strata, to the perfectly-joined pavement on the back side of the wee schoolhouse, the whole place is meant to convey emotions by hitting a kind of false pitch that only the tone-deaf can believe. It's like one of those psuedo-Armageddon theme parks in the Ozarks. It's painfully false. Looking up to the ridge above, or out at sidewalks beyond, I expect to see Bradford Pear trees and parking curbs. It's just so suburban.

But someone named Weitmann has done good work here, too. Walking back past the clapboard house, toward the main entrance, I pass half-a-dozen historic portraits or historical documents fixed right onto the side of the building. Inside the Nicodemus Historical Museum, we find links to info on Perry Bates, a broadside promising a Poor Man's Paradise for any young who are bold enough to Go West. A pleasant, open hall. There's even info about teff harvesting – a modern blue tractor managed by a modern Kansas farmer goes to work on one of our most ancient crops.

Between the museum and the library proper, there's a field of sunflowers, lots of plains-native trees and plants, and a fine little crop of morning glories lining the path into the main building. I go inside to see if I can find a librarian.

No luck. Tons of posters – even a link to the Governor's website (he's smiling down at visitors in a black suit and power tie) – but no librarians just now. There's a link to the Community Virtual Libraries Catalog, which opens a browser tab to the Alliance Virtual Libraries Catalog. This is a list of links on a Zoho wiki to about 120 SLURLs (*Second Life* URLs – map or location links to places on the grid). The 'catalog' is useless – like most other 'catalogs' you'll encounter in libraries inworld, because the SLURLs don't do anything but point your teleporter toward some other *Second Life* location. It's self-referential, and totally devoid of useful information. I walk over to a section for the Kansas Center for the Book. It's a bookshelf with cute little 19th-Century spine façades – but not one of them could you touch or read; not even the usual deposit of a URL or notecard into your inventory. Nothing.

The Cybrary City II Public Library, on the other hand, immediately proves its relative usefulness. Upon entry, the first thing I see is a big, bright, yellow sign above a bunch of books. It reads: Top 100 Gutenberg.org Downloaded Books (late January 2010) Click Here for a List of what is here so far. I try the second from the left – it's Vatsyayana's *Kama Sutra* translated by Captain Sir Richard Francis Burton. Now *that* could prove itself *useful*. Given, the 'book' only proffers up a hyperlink which takes you out to Project Gutenberg. Gutenberg is now icinged up with QR Codes, by the way, and it all makes me wonder why we need even a *good* library in *Second Life* – or why we need *Second Life* at all. But I digress; 'meet them where they're at', yo.

Academically speaking

Texas State University at San Marcos hosts a quaint little village of information kiosks in *Second Life*. There are models of original buildings, lovely shaded walkways, and even a version of the Albert B. Alkek library. This virtual library is designed well – the entrance and point of contact are clear and intuitive, though there's nobody manning the reference desk on a weekday afternoon, with Fall semester full in swing. To the right of the reference desk are periodical shelving with icons for the library's catalog, databases, contact info, and so on. Touching any of these will bring up the usual prompt: would you like to proceed to the URL? If yes, then the object opens a tab in your browser. There you are back at the Alkek website . . . on the Web . . . not in *Second Life*. The website itself (http://www.library.txstate.edu/), unlike this virtual library, is immediately useful.

Downstairs there's a fine, gray, quiet reading room. I linger for a little while, waiting to see if anyone shows up and browsing the portraits of past Texas statesmen (and stateswomen). Each portrait links out to the Web again (as the Ann Richards does, to her Wikipedia entry). I look for a while at her fine white hair and bright blue dress. Barbara Jordan. 'Ma' Ferguson.

No action

I mosey up to the roof, and sit on a golden chimera – a winged lion figure – to take in the scene. There's bloody *nothing happening* at Bobcat Village. I mean, this is the future, right? And this is virtual reality, right? And the ivory tower likes the virtual realities, right? So, where are all the college kids? Shouldn't they be lingering on low walls, reading Scott McCloud and sipping Purple Drank? Another bit of evidence that something is wrong with this entire model.

Where are the collegiate chats, sophomoric pranks, and drunken fights between freshers? The Bobcats built it, but no one came. You know what? The students and their profs are back in Real Life, arguing Hegel at Wake the Dead Coffee. They've got big plans to get real wired, hit Ranch Road 12 before sundown, and go see if they can find that old haunted stable off Purgatory Road.

Because *Second Life* sucks.

Public, as in Tammanial Hall

Back at Info Island (or *Second Life* Library, or Community Virtual Library, or whatever it's going to be called next), I take a look at the welcome signage. A bit cluttery, but nowhere near so bad as Kansas' attempt to welcome. One of the signs on a marquee is placed prominently and catches my eye: L.I.S. Student Union. Then it dawns on me – that's what all of this is; it's just one great big grant-magnet for graduate students.

I start bumbling around and walking into things. My stiff-forearmed, jerky stroll takes me up steps and down wide stony paths. I pause to breathe, purple hand on denim-textured hip. It's actually a lot of work, moving around in here.

Finally I'm at what seems to be the main library pavilion. The old library structure itself is gone, but there are a few folks – all librarians – hanging around here tonight. One's fresh from a costume contest, and she's back playing librarian while still wearing a fancy gray fox head. Puffy tail, white tipped. There's a short, brown lady with a floral print dress, and a thin, white Tina Fey type. I listen for a little while, then make conversation.

I ask about the place – the people who visit, the kinds of questions they ask. I get mild responses about 'educators' and people just 'wanting to find a quiet place' to be alone. Mostly they talk about toenail polish. No joke. 'The pink is nice,' etc. etc. I keep pestering them.

'Tarantula', the one in the dress, starts a private Instant Messaging exchange with me. She gives me the lowdown – this whole place is a sham. Not just the library areas, but *Second Life* itself. It's glam, it's glitz, it's sometimes sexy. But it is essentially hollow. She may have answered real reference questions 'once or twice' since she's been volunteering here, and Tarantula's been putting in the hours for a while. Her and Tina Fey both work real jobs as real librarians – Foxhead does too – but they come here after hours for volunteer shifts. They help Library and Information Science graduate students build exhibit halls. Tarantula takes me on a tour, and, sure, there's some nice builds to look at.

The whole system, she says, is pre-capitalistic. Without regulation and firm inworld contract law, lots of folks get scammed and burned. But your friends come from your business deals – and the intimation is that it's the same for inworld libraryland. You put in hours, you do the virtual reference desk, maybe you put together a nice faux-wood, faux-card, faux-catalog, and you get the chance to have your job description changed so that you can spend half your days here. Half your life.

I brush past low-hanging, crepe myrtle branches, all blooming in gauzy white, on my wide down wide steps. I'm baffled. All this work, all these hours, all this time spent away from Real Life . . . I ask Tarantula why she invests in a world that doesn't offer real service to real people.

'Because I can't build a competitor,' she says, and trots off to the next sodium-lit exhibition space.

She believes in virtual worlds, and she believes in libraries. Both are great equalizers and, as she sees it, great educators. But *Second Life* has become a spot to work on dance moves with bare-breasted Final Fantasy characters at Club XxesS. It's not serious.

It's not serious.

I'm a Mac. And I'm a PC

I turn up another time at the Community Virtual Library pavilion. A weeknight, primetime, and nobody's home. I sit on a wall for a while, then figure, what the hell? I sit down behind the reference desk and study the place. Wide, teal, roundish furniture. Complex red and black rug design. A fake cat.

A few minutes later, I get a taker. A Cheetarah-looking club-girl called 'The Pleiadian' is suddenly in front of me. Tight jeans.

'Hi,' I say. 'Can I help you find anything?'

'Hi. Sure', she says. Her Mac won't load *Second Life* right.

I give her the usual liability bit, then suggest she uninstall *Second Life*, then re-install it.

'Will I still be here,' she asks, shifting her hips, 'or will I be in Third Life? Heehe.'

':-) You'll disappear during the uninstall, temporarily,' I say.

'But my inventory and stuff?'

'All fine. All that's tied to your account, on a Linden server farm somewhere.'

I ask her about *Second Life*, and the library. I tell her I'm not with the actual library inworld . . . just watching and chatting with folks. She's a librarian, too, actually, and says that new folks here have to shadow an established Community Virtual Library team member.

'I'll check out your Mac suggestion,' she says, 'with a real librarian. You could be anyone. See you later.'

'Sister,' I say, 'I *am* anyone. Hahaha.' But it's too late. She's teleported away.

So I chill again for a little bit, waiting for somebody to wander in. Eventually a cowboy, 'Balboa' joins me.

'You the usual?' I ask. 'The regular volunteer?'

He was. I offered the seat at the reference desk, but we just stood around chatting. I told him that I just couldn't get my head around *Second Life*, or its libraries.

'Well,' he said, 'in a community library, a public library, people come in with questions, right? And you answer those questions, which are usually about the community. They live in a community. It's like that here. Only the community is *Second Life*. People want to know where to find cowboy boots, and real estate profiles just like in real life. You serve the community.'

That, I told him, was the best answer I'd ever heard for that question.

Balboa and I chatted for a while. He told me about the professional discussions of Banned Books Week, of pragmatic workshops on dealing with patrons wishing to challenge a book, and even of a chat he had with a wily security guard from British Columbia who explained the 4th dimension to him by way of a quick build: a line drawing in four colors of a slowly spinning tesseract. *Second Life* and its libraries, Balboa firmly believes, is a worthy project.

His time working on a state library's inworld presence paid off by getting some *Second Life* patrons to contact him through Real Life e-mail and IM.

I would have given the man's hand a good hard shake, if I could have. I would have clasped him on the shoulder and looked him in the eyes and said *thank you, sir*. Here was a man who *got it*, and who'd said what I had long hoped I would hear from *somebody* in this play-pretend land of dress-up and dawdle. Here was a man who tied virtual worlds to service at his reference desk – more so, at least, than anybody else I'd met in a virtual world so far.

Here was a man who had his head screwed on straight.

Maybe there was potential here after all.

Real Life again

Balboa had to go tend to a grandchild. The Pleiadian had to go refill her teacup and reboot her husband's MacBook. Tarantula, Tina Fey, all the folks in Waterhead or at 'da club' or riding rocket-powered freight trains in Steampunk communities . . . all of these folks eventually had to get up from their machines and go fix a sandwich, let the dog out, take a shower, set the alarm clock. They all had to brush teeth, go to the toilet, and clip their toenails.

For all the exuberance and excitement about chatting with pixelated avatars in parallax, or flying in false starships, or grooming fellow cosplayers at digiRevi or The Furry Cuddle Cave & Mystic Dreams Main Store . . . we all eventually must come back to our Real bodies in the here and now sometime.

The question remains: what happens then?

7

After virtual worlds

Abstract: The development of virtual worlds through web browser interfaces is only one step in the development of virtual realities. Augmented reality, the pairing of information layers with our perception of actual objects in the Real World, is the next major development. Phones and other personal information devices are becoming platforms for hybrid experiences that combine elements of the virtual and Real. Libraries will have to develop strategies for service in and documentation of augmented reality experiences.

Key words: augmented reality, phones, tablets, gestural interface, virtual services.

Augmented reality is already making waves in information services. QR Codes and Stickybits are both good examples of bridges between physical objects in the Real World and mediated virtual objects.

Phones are everywhere (and *everyware* as Adam Greenfield might have it), and we've had quite a shift in the last five years in terms of how library administration has viewed phones and phone-like devices. Libraries have been forced to cede ground to cell phones, and within a few years what was once very much like a phone has become something more like a little bitty laptop. Wifi or 4G? Whatever gets the job done.

There has been a marked increase in students using phones in academic libraries, of course, but what is perhaps more surprising is that they have begun to use the phones to access library resources. Perhaps a dozen times in the last year, a patron has come up to the reference desk in my own college library and flashed a little gray-white LCD screen at me, asking 'can you help me find this book?' Instead of searching the catalog, jotting the call number on a notepad, then going to the stacks – we go right to the stacks to find the call number that's up on the screen. They're also stepping into databases this way.

The chatter and buzz and hype about phones as *everyware* has finally given way to the very undramatic and anti-climatic practice of using phones and similar gizmos (wifi pads, etc.) to get to whatever information may be needed. It's just daily practice, now.

Phones are changing. They're shifting from things-for-talking, into things that deliver apps. 'Apps' are specialized Internet tools that let you do very particular and limited jobs. You may think of a specialized need: maybe you need to find a parking spot, get a date, find true north, or figure some stoichiometry real quick. Word is, 'there's an app for that'. Apps aren't general tools, they are specific and very limited in scope.

As the voice communication aspect of phones become less important in light of text communication and the rise of apps, we see more and more novel apps in development. But the apps that tie your place, your identity, and your social networks together are perhaps the most useful and popular – geolocative, real-time, augmented reality applications let you see an information-rich version of the street in front of you layered with detail about places and people you want to know about.

Using a phone's camera, an augmented reality app (like Layar, a Dutch company launched in 2009) can lay information about the place you're seeing through the lens right on top of your live view of a scene. Using GPS and optical cues, the augmented reality app can push icons into the viewscreen on your phone that are relevant for your current position in space. YouTube has a Layar app that lets its users see videos – the videos that were filmed in or near the exact spot the user is now standing. This means you can look down the length of Elysian Fields to your north, then pull out your phone and see that same scene, but with icons for any videos of doings between Chartres and Burgundy pegged to locations on the live image right in front of you.

There are endless ways to set information layering onto live, Real World scenes. Stanbeelden is an app that shows 'information about statues located in Belgium.' Your City 100 Years Ago ports in archival photographs and layers them onto your current position. Augmented reality apps exist for tracing taxi routes in Paris, getting coupons delivered to your phone as you walk by the retailers offering them, running playful war tactics with friends in the suburbs, and pushing reviews of tourist spots as you travel India. All real time, all sensitive to your position in space. This marriage of Internet to Real waking life is more than (and very different from) virtual reality; these tools augment your actual living experiences.

Augmented reality (and there's bound to be a smooth bit of neologism slang for the idea soon – for now, here on out, we'll call it *layered reality*, *layers*, or *layering* after the company mentioned above) provides a number of rich opportunities for the enterprising information professional or organization. Some of the examples above (coupons, tourist reviews, gaming) are poised to make big money for their developers. Let's consider some of the broader arcs for information dynamics.

Big database vendors layering packets on top of actual geography could do a lot to further engagement with the content of articles. News items, editorials, and peer-reviewed research related to the 1995 heat-related deaths in North Lawndale, Chicago, come tumbling down onto your multi-touch screen as you cruise up Pulaski Road between Ogden and 290. Corner groceries mentioned in evening news transcripts glow on your screen as you pass. A renovated duplex flares in familiar blue, a surname glowing above the brown roof: not the name of the current resident, but the name of an elderly African-American lady (one of hundreds) who over-heated or dehydrated in the same house, twenty years before. If big vendors won't layer this information, maybe an entreprenurial ex-librarian will get hold of briefly-open APIs and do it herself.

History research would certainly change with all of history spilling out before you on your phone – everywhere you step, you feel the need to leap a pile of dung, give berth to a bristling cowhand, or take the long way around a rail trolley station that no longer exists. Even if only the commonly-owned material (public domain, patent office records, Works Program Administration photographs, government press releases) were layered onto real-time walk-through views of downtown Dallas, Texas, there'd be an impossible amount to sort through. But even if the layered view were facet-spun to show only public records related to the assassination of John Fitzgerald Kennedy, any stroll from Deep Elum to 35-East, or from Dealy to the railyard south of I-30 would present views so thick with data and text that a researcher could spend weeks tying names and faces from November 1963 to places and organizations still in existence. History could be moved through *live*, historians running as spiders, spinning lines of webwork between previously unnoticed intimations and yet-living bank accounts. It's like having a Jim Marrs in your shirt pocket.

Health trends, real estate values, amoebic upticks, vandalism patterns, temporary price-cuts at butcher shops: all the data, with the right kinds of layering applications, may be laid out by the scrupulous information pro, and offered for a price. Who else is going to do it? And someone will want to pay.

Data, articles, information – it all has to be made attractive, if it's going to sell. The fact that information is mostly *un*attractive is why librarians and researchers have jobs in the first place. If it were fun to work with, it'd be play. If it were play, everybody would want to do it. Lots of money will be made by making all this hard work into play (or at least into something that can be engaged playfully). The Edward Tufte and Andrew Vande Moere sensibilities will rule, not only because of the fine aesthetic (beauty) they may lead us to, but also because beauty that leads to truth is very cash-actionable.

But, then again, maybe this is giving away the store.

Thumbing into new turf

Physical pushes into virtual spaces might also be considered a type of augmented reality, though reversed from the usual orientation of virtual objects floating in Real space and time.

There are several interesting examples of this, and since the advent of multi-touch displays (now common in smartphones) the idea of a more intimate movement of the body into online, informational, or virtual spaces is becoming accepted and, perhaps, expected. The glaring smears of grease and sweat, rubbed in fancy runs across my iPod Touch, remind me that I and the machine are a lot closer than I think. Thought and word and deed are boiled down into a single momentous moment of *touch*. I connect with the wider world (through games, e-mail, text messages, and novel app vectors) with a slickly biological pattern of bursting oily streaks on the multi-touch display, lines reminescent of some Zaha Hadid sketch. I now *touch* the Web when I want to know something. The machine and I are both actors in an immediate and physical network, and in the broader network of e-mail, apps, games, and the Web.

This movement of my body into cyberspace, even in such a halting and wanting form, is startling to me. I think we'll look back at this moment some years from now with a startled and stomach-churning astonishment – the moment we stopped asking silly virtual animations (alzheimer-ish polygons staggering through iterating and perfect blue-white skies) to make appearances in our world, and finally started making appearances in theirs.

Two examples stand out and deserve discussion in some detail.

I've not yet experienced gestural interface firsthand, at least beyond anything as simple as multi-touch. But maybe you've seen the SixthSense TED Talks with Pattie Maes and Pranav Mistry (of MIT's Fluid Interfaces Group) shooting the Web out of their chests and fingering it on plain pieces of paper. When we talk objects, Mistry says in one video demonstration, we're obliged to talk about gestures. By turning everyday objects into media, Maes, Mistry, and their team at MIT (Tangible Media Group) have made gestural gateways into the everyday world of physical touch and movement.

John Underkoffler's work is thematically very similar, although his work on gestural interface is focused more on interaction with the wholly virtual. Maes and Mistry's work turns physical objects into interfaces, while Underkoffler ramps up traditional interface with *screens* to new and exciting levels. Underkoffler's version invites us to move through globes of icons, and spinning streams of graphics orbiting cores of concepts; it's a kind of kinetic and memetic astrolabe through fields of human-readable information.

Underkoffler was a consultant to Steven Spielberg for the film *Minority Report*, which featured near-future police using advanced somatic interfaces to pull information from security cameras, newspaper archives, and other kinds of information sources. The cops would work in a kind of machine-readable sign language, pulling and pushing documents and menus, and scrolling through vast fields of visualized data. Underkoffler and his team are now able to demonstrate a working model for this interface – it's no longer sicence fiction, no longer just in the movies. In his 2010 *TED Talk*, Underkoffler said that 'The gloves go away in a matter of months or years . . .' – referring to the slim glove-like devices that stretch from wrist to fingertips. The gloves have visual targets, similar in *concept* to the ping-pong balls or high-contrast tape actors wear in the filming of 'green screen' computer-generated effects. When Chris Anderson asked him about the status of the technology five years out for access by the general consumer, Undkeroffler said, 'I think in five years time, when you buy a computer, you'll get this.'

G-Speak is the system that makes all this work. The *Inventor of the Week* series highlights Underkoffler's work on this. 'Also based on work done while pursuing his PhD, Underkoffler designed a gestural interface system that came to be known as G-Speak, which allows users to navigate and interact with data in an unprecedented, visually rich, natural and responsive manner. G-Speak would interpret a user's motion to move through datasets without him or her needing to use a computer mouse or any other physical object to do so' (2007).

G-Speak is an operating system and an interface. Underkoffler says the two things are one and the same, and should no longer be understood as different aspects of computing. In describing Apple's early success with the Macintosh, and their need to design a new operating system, he points out that we've forgotten something very important: 'The OS *is* the interface; the interface *is* the OS. It's like the Land and the King in [the legend of King] Arthur – they are inseparable. They are one.' With the incredible ramping up of software abilities, hardware power, and the awesome volumes of data generated since the Macintosh, he suggests, it's high time to interact with our machines in new ways. G-Speak 'explain space' to machines, and thereby allows people to interact more intuitively (that is, bodily) with information. All this is so that the Real World 'merges with the simulation.' Physical Boolean operations, using hands to part and sort clumps of data-objects into useful categories, becomes commonplace.

Accelerometers on smartphones are just a tiny first taste of the physically-interactive changes that are to come for popular consumer electronics. As this field of gestural interface grows and matures, again, 'virtual' worlds will be less interesting, less meaningful, and less useful for modeling and communication. Knowing virtual worlds well *now*, as information professionals, before these changes take root, places us in a much more confident position when it comes time for us to classify, organize, and make accessible new breeds of data, documents, and chimeric online ephemera for our future clients.

Maes speaks about SixthSense technology as metadata oriented. The point is to give people access to tools that allow them to know things about the things they find and use in Real Life . . .

Siftables, another MIT Media Lab project, are sort of semi-intelligent blocks that allow users to do things with images, audio, video, and games by moving the 'siftable' block pieces in relation to each other. Demonstrations show educational and artistic applications – blocks representing numbers get stacked, flipped, and slid out of range all to reinforce arithmetical lessons tactilely. Blocks representing colors pour virtual paint into blocks representing buckets – mixtures form and flicker so that what would be hexadecimal codes are seen live by naked eye. And blocks can be instruments. This one a drum machine, this one some treble, that one a set of haunting strings, another a harpsichord riff: pulling and tilting them speeds tempo, while stacking might tie one instrument's rhythm to that of the bottom-most block's.

Wii, Guitar Hero, Dance Dance Revolution . . . maybe even Duck Hunt and all its post-1984 progeny; these games took the Real World (your body, your hands, your floor, your friends) and mashed them up with a virtual stage, dancefloor, swamp, yoga studio, or bowling alley. Less ethereal, maybe, than the Kenobi-like wand-and-mind gestural interfaces of SixthSense or *Minority Report*, these games depend on in-rail light-guns, PixArt optical sensor circuitry, pressure-sensitive dance pads, and low-power three-axis ADXL330 accelerometers. Your body does stuff (stuff remeniscent of analog Atari games – sore thumbs and all) to machines that are often offline (and, in any case, find no need to be online to complete the tasks at hand). The game gets played.

The testing, tinting, and blending in little bits at a time: this all affects our expectations and changes the culture of information retrieval. We become accustomed to doing more with our flesh to get more out of our machines. The activities of research, play, surfing, browsing, and searching become truly holistic endeavors. It's getting to the point, now, that I find not being able to get a response when I tap liquid crystal displays annoying and stifling. I still need a mouse and a keyboard? Really?

It is increasingly often that we log in somatically and mentally, and that we invest physically and emotionally when we have to deal with machines and visualized information.

8

Conclusions

We've covered a lot of ground, and I want to end this book with some thoughts on where we go from here.

In the last chapter, we looked at augmented reality and what it's doing for markets and organizations already. The ground is well prepared for the transformations to come – as the Web is dying (well . . . sort of. See the debate about Web v. Apps after the WIRED of September 2010) and specific, selective applications grow in importance and in number of users, augmented reality tools have a perfect medium for spreading now: apps on your phone or tablet.

What will a post-virtual or blended-virtual/Real World look like? We can't guess (futurism is a shady business – even Bruce Sterling will tell you that . . .). But we can sketch out how we'll need to change to accommodate new information-seeking behaviors in such worlds, at least in the rough.

The future isn't in *Second Life*, *World of Warcraft*, or any of it. *Farmville*, *Civilization* – there will always be games and distractions, however social, geolocative, or integrated into other aspects of your life they become. *EVE Online* will never let you feel freefall.

But in their ability to connect us to others in the fields of our own imaginations, games and virtual worlds empower us beyond anything a ticket to ride on Virgin Galactic can offer. When the virtual and the Real become consciously integrated and purposefully (maybe self-effacingly) self-aware, our clients and patrons will have something perhaps more precious than good search technique or searing knowledge of advanced query syntax. They'll have the power to create worlds within worlds, and to create new worlds out of old ones. They will be empowered to translate their own daily-lived experiences into something that is at once numinous and floating, and also canny and embodied.

These new semi-virtual worlds will be useful metaphors for rendering daily Real Life problems and worries into new and novel contexts. Their semi-Real lives will be active testlabs for running useful and fictitious hacks for the odd and banal problems affecting Real people with Real bodies in Real space and time. Shaving nicks. Stops for petrol. Mis-remembered postal codes. A son's skinned knee. Schlepping eggshells out to the compost heap. A low tire, again. The wrong key, again. The *fucking* cat at 4 AM!

Information professionals may still find ready work as teachers – folks will always need to know new things about how to find, access, and glean the actionable information from the floating petabytes of data all around them. But less traditional services are also waiting in the umbral zones where worlds overlap.

As virtual world models sharpen to approach the resolution of something more like the Real World, our clients and patrons may require expert help in sorting virtual ontologies from the laws of Real Life. The laws of physics, of information dynamics, of social-actor behavior – all may work differently in a virtual environment. But if that virtual environment approaches the Real in the intensity of its illusion, confusion about which laws apply in which contexts may begin to set in. Information professionals could become *handlers* for those of our clients who find one world psychologically bleeding into another, or who find the Real World dissolving around them as they try to keep accounts straight in many worlds at once.

Economic and business research services take on new dimensions when virtual currencies have to be traded between multiple worlds. Warcraft Gold and Lindens don't trade on the same markets. But once folded into Real World RMB, Pounds Sterling, or US Dollars, a virtual chit can become any other kind of chit we might want it to. Cross-world marketing research could lead to insights about brand and meme thematic repetition in storefronts across worlds – a lucrative corner, if you can convince the right entrepreneurs you're good at spotting the colors that 'work' in worlds that work.

And, when it's all boiled down, we're talking about worlds that are by-and-large *social.* Certainly the Real World is, and is becoming more so. Any augmented reality hybrids we end up with will be social too, dense as beehives. Your clients will be looking for *people.* Information professionals adept at following the slim traces of personal movement both in and between worlds will find gigs aplenty. We all want to find others, and we all want to be found by *somebody*, sometimes. Gum-shoeing ain't going nowhere, as they say.

As we prepare for these changes and sublimations of Real into Virtual into Augemented realities, we do well to remember that information dynamics in virtual worlds can be understood best by studying information dynamics in the world at hand. Whatever shape the future takes, if it is in any part virtual it will also be by measures *augmented*, *Real*, *messy*, *dramatic*, *disappointing*, and *amazing*. Just like Real Life.

Because, at the end of the day, virtual worlds are intimately joined to our Real lives.

Appendix I: SL librarianship

The following is a set of sample raw chat transcripts from general meeting places in *Second Life* and from *Second Life* library areas. These interactions form the basis for some of the episodes in Chapter 6, but I've included only a small sample of chat transcriptions here. This is some of the best, and some of the worst, and all of this is from Summer and Fall 2010. Names have been changed to protect privacy.

[2010/08/12 14:10] *#5*: please retouch to get your tp.
[2010/08/12 14:11] *Greeter*: Welcome to the Michigan Library Consortium. If you have any questions, please IM Evie Mikazuki and she will get back with you shortly.
[2010/08/12 14:12] *SL Library Monitor 1.3* whispers: the term is '-2'
[2010/08/12 14:13] *SL Library Monitor 1.3* whispers: done searching. . .
[2010/08/12 14:16] *SL Library Monitor 1.5* whispers: OCLC Digital Collections Management = *http://www.mlcnet.org/cms/sitem.cfm/library_tools/software/contentdm/*
[2010/08/12 14:16] *SL Library Monitor 1.5* whispers: =
[2010/08/12 14:16] *SL Library Monitor 1.5* whispers: =
[2010/08/12 14:16] *MLC Monitor 1.3* whispers: Web Page: 6:
[2010/08/12 14:16] *SL Library Monitor 1.5* whispers: =
[2010/08/12 14:16] *MLC Monitor 1.3* whispers: MLC Home Page = *http://www.mlcnet.org*
[2010/08/12 14:17] *MeL Monitor 1.3* whispers: Web Page: 3:
[2010/08/12 14:17] *SL Library Monitor 1.5* whispers: eJournals = *http://www.mlcnet.org/cms/sitem.cfm/databases_econtent/ejournals/*
[2010/08/12 14:17] *MeL Monitor 1.3* whispers: Michigan eLibrary Workshops = *http://portal.mlcnet.org/cms/sitem.cfm/workshops_conferences/mel_workshops/*

[2010/08/12 14:26] *FW Visitor Greeter TP v2.0*: Welcome to Gold Country Library, Woody. Were brand new, and hope to have interesting materials from throughout the beautiful and historic California Gold Rush Country! Please take your time and look around.
[2010/08/12 14:41] Teleport completed from CAVE (0,46,25)
[2010/08/12 14:43] *caleidoscopio43X Yokosuka*: Vaya horas, como el no curra
[2010/08/12 14:45] *saraines 3lan*: español
[2010/08/12 14:47] Teleport completed from Waterhead (87,99,38)
[2010/09/26 19:17] *Woody Evans*: Here's one for the record. This place is not useful.

[18:48] *Women in* Second Life: The information you requested is in a new folder named Women in *Second Life* in your inventory.
[18:50] *Woody Evans*: Hi.
[18:50] *Sashimi Max*: Hi Woody
[18:51] *Woody Evans*: I'm checking out SL Library again. It's been a while.
[18:51] *Sashimi Max*: great!
[18:51] *Sashimi Max*: it keeps changing
[18:51] *Woody Evans*: What is it for? Is it just for librarians and LIS students?
[18:52] *Sashimi Max*: it's open for anyone to come learn and expore
[18:53] *Woody Evans*: I'm stuck! Nice helmet. Is it a fox or what?
[18:53] *Sashimi Max*: can you keep walking
[18:53] *Sashimi Max*: I just came froma costume contest
[18:54] *Sashimi Max*: it's the wolf
[18:54] *Sashimi Max*: from whre the wild things are
[18:54] *Sashimi Max*: r u still stuck?
[18:54] *Woody Evans*: I think I'll teleport back to the Unon, walk over again . . .
[18:54] *Sashimi Max*: k
[18:55] Try moving closer. Can't sit on object because it is not in the same region as you.
[18:55] *Sashimi Max*: uh oh
[18:55] Teleport completed from Info Island (76,2,32)
[18:55] *Isabelle LegoGeek*: excuse you mav
[18:55] *Waffle*: Everybody goes into their IMs
[18:55] Teleport completed from Waterhead (35,75,25)
[18:56] *Mamacita Tarantula*: OK . . .
[18:56] *Fake Tina Fey Fall*: hello Mamacita

[18:56] *Mamacita Tarantula*: Hello Woody.
[18:56] *Sonya-TT Tidewater*: Hi Woody
[18:56] *Woody Evans*: Hi all
[18:56] *Fake Tina Fey Fall*: psst. dont say anything but that guy over there is purple.
[18:56] *Fake Tina Fey Fall*: hehe
[18:57] *Sonya-TT Tidewater*: LOL
[18:57] *Woody Evans*: Cool skirt, Mamacita
[18:57] *Woody Evans*: Hi Sashi.
[18:57] *Sonya-TT Tidewater*: Hi Sashimi
[18:57] *Fake Tina Fey Fall*: I dont see a sashi. where?
[18:57] *Sonya-TT Tidewater*: I'm getting ready to leave, but Mamacita can help you if you need it
[18:58] *Fake Tina Fey Fall*: ok
[18:58] *Woody Evans*: I'm writing a book, and I wonder if anybody would like to chat about SL libraries.
[18:58] *Fake Tina Fey Fall*: I havent been back to SL for over a year.
[18:58] *Fake Tina Fey Fall*: I missed the library here.
[18:59] *Sonya-TT Tidewater*: I'm sure the people who manage CVL would like to talk to you, Woody.
[18:59] *Fake Tina Fey Fall*: glad I decided to download it again and visit
[18:59] *Woody Evans*: My first time here in a while
[18:59] *Sonya-TT Tidewater*: It has changed, but the people here are still friendly.
[18:59] *Fake Tina Fey Fall*: yes. It has changed so very much.
[18:59] *Mamacita Tarantula*: Welcome back.
[18:59] *Fake Tina Fey Fall*: I am not sure how to get around anymore
[18:59] *Woody Evans*: I've talked with [a founding member of *Second Life* Library] but it's been a while. a year I guess.
[19:00] *Fake Tina Fey Fall*: TY Mamacita.
[19:00] *Fake Tina Fey Fall*: Love your color Woody. my fav
[19:00] *Mamacita Tarantula*: Click Move on the bottom of your screen and pull the move arrows up so they don't disappear every time you click something else.
[19:00] *Sonya-TT Tidewater*: She has changed jobs, Woody.
[19:00] *Mamacita Tarantula*: [She is really] HyperPatient right.
[19:01] *Woody Evans*: Oh Sonya. . I'm out of date now. . not with ALS anymore?
[19:01] *Sonya-TT Tidewater*: No, [she has a different username].
[19:01] *Mamacita Tarantula*: OK . . . .
[19:01] *Woody Evans*: I gotta sit somewhere. My abs are killin me.

[19:01] *Sonya-TT Tidewater*: HyperPatient is Sammy Ramtha.
[19:01] *Woody Evans*: Flight always gets me in the abs.
[19:01] *Mamacita Tarantula*: And I'm [real name].
[19:01] *Fake Tina Fey Fall*: what do you mean about the arros Mamacita?
[19:01] *Mamacita Tarantula*: [personal URL]
[19:02] *Mamacita Tarantula*: I mean if you click move, your movement controlls appear.
[19:02] *Sonya-TT Tidewater*: Thanks Mamacita
[19:02] *Fake Tina Fey Fall*: ahh. ok
[19:02] *Mamacita Tarantula*: You can side step and jump. They finally put that back in Version 2
[19:02] *Woody Evans*: So who comes to this library, this CVL?
[19:02] *Sonya-TT Tidewater*: I need to go. Nice meeting you.
[19:02] *Mamacita Tarantula*: Have a great night.
[19:02] *Sonya-TT Tidewater*: I'll let Mamacita tell you. :)
[19:02] *Woody Evans*: You too,, bye
[19:02] *Fake Tina Fey Fall*: oh. you too Sonya.
[19:03] *Fake Tina Fey Fall*: woody, your sitting in air
[19:03] *Mamacita Tarantula*: What are you sitting on Woody?
[19:03] *Mamacita Tarantula*: So how's it going Tina?
[19:03] *Fake Tina Fey Fall*: well, I cannot seem to get my feet looking right.
[19:04] *Mamacita Tarantula*: They look fine to me.
[19:04] *Fake Tina Fey Fall*: and, the chat is filling up my screen so I cannot hardly see you two
[19:04] *Woody Evans*: Hell, I just sat down. Dunno.
[19:04] *Mamacita Tarantula*: Do you have your advanced options on?
[19:04] *Fake Tina Fey Fall*: I have to keep minimizing the chat to see
[19:04] *Mamacita Tarantula*: You even have pink toes.
[19:04] *Fake Tina Fey Fall*: this all looks so different from when I was last here
[19:04] *Mamacita Tarantula*: Do a front view on the view controls and zoom in. I'm assuming you are a Viewer 2 user.
[19:05] *Fake Tina Fey Fall*: Love pink . . . . and purple.
[19:05] *Mamacita Tarantula*: They'are a very tasteful pale pink.
[19:05] *Fake Tina Fey Fall*: next month is Breast Cancer awaremness month. Go pink!
[19:05] *Mamacita Tarantula*: Ctrl-alt-D turns on your advanced options.
[19:05] *Fake Tina Fey Fall*: I really dont even know HOW my toes got pink
[19:06] *Mamacita Tarantula*: Are you wearing 'fake feet?'

[19:06] *Woody Evans*: Monday night . . . you guys get any patrons in here on weeknights?
[19:06] *Fake Tina Fey Fall*: Ctrl-alt-D didnt do anything
[19:06] *Mamacita Tarantula*: Toe nails and fingernails come with your skin.
[19:06] *Mamacita Tarantula*: Not this late, but sometimes we do.
[19:07] *Fake Tina Fey Fall*: oh
[19:07] *Fake Tina Fey Fall*: but my shoes are not right.
[19:07] *Mamacita Tarantula*: Yes it did, look up to see if you either have or have lost your Advanced tab.
[19:07] *Mamacita Tarantula*: It's on top of your window.
[19:07] *Fake Tina Fey Fall*: they are not fitting
[19:07] *Mamacita Tarantula*: They look fine to me.
[19:07] *Mamacita Tarantula*: What's wrong with them?
[19:07] *Woody Evans*: Mind if I ask (is for my research), WHO are the patrons? What kind of stuff do they want to know?
[19:07] *Fake Tina Fey Fall*: oh! I do see advance now
[19:08] *Mamacita Tarantula*: They are mostly library school students, librarians, and educators.
[19:08] *Mamacita Tarantula*: Sometimes they want to find a place.
[19:08] *Mamacita Tarantula*: Other times they want to go somewhere where there is people.
[19:08] *Mamacita Tarantula*: Often they just want to be left alone.
[19:08] *Fake Tina Fey Fall*: Are you really a librarian?
[19:08] *Mamacita Tarantula*: Once or twice, I've had a 'real life' reference question.
[19:08] *Woody Evans*: Mamacita, a place in SL?
[19:08] *Mamacita Tarantula*: Yes . . . .
[19:08] *Fake Tina Fey Fall*: How bout you Woody?
[19:08] *Mamacita Tarantula*: Yes, they have to go to a class or a meeting.
[19:09] *Mamacita Tarantula*: http://facstaff.gpc.edu/~ekramer
[19:09] *Woody Evans*: I mean, they want to 'find a place' in SL?
[19:09] *Fake Tina Fey Fall*: there are classes here?
[19:09] *Mamacita Tarantula*: That's my personal professional page.
[19:09] *Woody Evans*: Yep, librarian at a college in TX.
[19:09] *Mamacita Tarantula*: Earlier in the evening and during the day. SJSU's program is based in *Second Life*.
[19:09] *Fake Tina Fey Fall*: cool. Arent Librarians awesome!
[19:10] *Mamacita Tarantula*: We try . . .
[19:10] *Fake Tina Fey Fall*: I love being a librarian
[19:10] *Woody Evans*: Hmm. I hope so. No doubt we all are. But where are the people for this world?

[19:10] *Woody Evans*: I mean, whereare th problems, th questons, the service, the contact?
[19:10] *Woody Evans*: (I'm an SL skeptic . . .)
[19:10] *Mamacita Tarantula*: The people are spread out. Population density of Wyoming.
[19:11] *Fake Tina Fey Fall*: Thats what I was wondering Woody. There does not seem to be much traffic in SL
[19:11] *Mamacita Tarantula*: If you want people, I can give you a landmark for Dance Island or half a dozen loud, dance parties.
[19:11] *Fake Tina Fey Fall*: not like it was last year anyway.
[19:11] *Fake Tina Fey Fall*: maybe its just because it's monday
[19:11] *Mamacita Tarantula*: Some will play oldies, some play house music, and some play reggeaton.
[19:11] *Woody Evans*: Why are librarians here, then?
[19:12] *Mamacita Tarantula*: I get professional points for this at my job.
[19:12] *Mamacita Tarantula*: Also sometimes you really get to help people.
[19:12] *Fake Tina Fey Fall*: really? how does that work Mamacita
[19:12] *Mamacita Tarantula*: For a long time, this was my only job in SL.
[19:12] *Fake Tina Fey Fall*: job?
[19:12] *Mamacita Tarantula*: Yes . . . . Look at the web page.
[19:12] *Fake Tina Fey Fall*: I want to have a job here
[19:12] *Fake Tina Fey Fall*: in SL
[19:12] *Mamacita Tarantula*: I'm a real life academic librarian.
[19:13] *Mamacita Tarantula*: They're hard to come by unless you know the righ tpeople.
[19:13] *Fake Tina Fey Fall*: I'm a public librarian
[19:13] *Mamacita Tarantula*: Are you a librarian Tina, because if you are, we have plenty of reference slots left.
[19:13] *Fake Tina Fey Fall*: How do I find Mr. or Mrs. Right?
[19:13] *Mamacita Tarantula*: OK, then sign yourself up. I think they are having the orientation very soon.
[19:13] *Fake Tina Fey Fall*: sign up where?
[19:13] *Mamacita Tarantula*: You need to IM Rolig Loon.
[19:14] *Mamacita Tarantula*: Let me see the notice about Orientation.
[19:16] *Mamacita Tarantula*: I don't see it, but I think the orientation is this Saturday.
[19:16] *Woody Evans*: Mamacita, I'm accustomed to 2800+ visitors per day (door count). . lots of lit crit questions, lots of social issues stuff. database instuction . . .
[19:16] *Woody Evans*: can you give me a sample of ref questions here?
[19:16] *Mamacita Tarantula*: Sounds like a liberal arts college or a university.

[19:17] *Fake Tina Fey Fall*: ☺
[19:17] *Fake Tina Fey Fall*: Mamacita, may I add you?
[19:17] *Woody Evans*: it's a community college. 2 yr degrees.
[19:18] *Woody Evans*: a darn busy one.
[19:18] *Mamacita Tarantula*: I work at a community college too. I do tons of computer trouble shooting.
[19:18] *Mamacita Tarantula*: Here we don't get the traffic.
[19:18] *Mamacita Tarantula*: But most of SL is empty.
[19:18] *Mamacita Tarantula*: You know what happens when it doesn't get empty.
[19:19] *Woody Evans*: Why should libraries be in this empty place?
[19:19] *Mamacita Tarantula*: Because you know what full ones are like?
[19:20] *Woody Evans*: Is this an escape?
[19:20] *Mamacita Tarantula*: No, but you don't have land and neighbors.
[19:20] *Fake Tina Fey Fall*: I know our library can get crazy
[19:20] *Mamacita Tarantula*: You don't go to clubs either . . . Think lag.
[19:20] *Fake Tina Fey Fall*: Mamacita, may I add yoU?
[19:20] *Mamacita Tarantula*: Also, with neighbors you get people who act like pigs.
[19:21] *Mamacita Tarantula*: You can't go for a walk . . . Ban lines, security orbs . . . .
[19:21] *Mamacita Tarantula*: Huge jungle walls.
[19:21] *Woody Evans*: Mamacita – in RL or SL?
[19:21] *Mamacita Tarantula*: Even if we were in a busy spot, people might not be able to reach us.
[19:21] *Woody Evans*: OH, I see. No, I meant is this an escape from RL libraries?
[19:22] *Fake Tina Fey Fall*: I should hope not
[19:23] *Fake Tina Fey Fall*: I IM'd her
[19:25] *Fake Tina Fey Fall*: Mamacita?
[19:26] *Mamacita Tarantula*: I'll be back . . . . I'm sorry for the private conversation, Tina.
[19:26] *Fake Tina Fey Fall*: woody.
[19:26] *Mamacita Tarantula*: You're welcome to come with us.
[19:26] *Fake Tina Fey Fall*: to where?
[19:26] *Woody Evans*: Hi Tina
[19:26] *Woody Evans*: Let's go!
[19:26] *Mamacita Tarantula*: The exhibit halls.
[19:26] *Mamacita Tarantula*: They're right in front of me.
[19:26] *Mamacita Tarantula*: There's one on the right and one on the left.
[19:27] *Mamacita Tarantula*: OK, to my left is a dance floor and a hot tub.

[19:27] *Mamacita Tarantula*: The dances are Greek and on individual pose balls.
[19:29] *Mamacita Tarantula*: Some of this is really well built.
[19:30] *Woody Evans*: do these OA journals open in a web browser
[19:30] *Mamacita Tarantula*: My favorite one is the math and science one in here and the astronomy one in the building across the way.
[19:30] *Mamacita Tarantula*: Yes, the OA journals open in a web browser.
[19:32] *Mamacita Tarantula*: Of course we have a library science exhibit.
[19:33] *Teleporter – Up*: Please right-click and select Teleport
[19:21] *Mamacita Tarantula*: Do you want honest answers about this place?
[19:22] *Woody Evans*: yes indeed.
[19:22] *Mamacita Tarantula*: OK, I don't want to lose this volunteer positiion so we can use my personal email.
[19:22] *Mamacita Tarantula*: Do you have a personal email or even your job one.
[19:23] *Mamacita Tarantula*: This is a reference question and it's protected by confidentiality.
[19:23] *Woody Evans*: sounds good. I'll keep it anonymous. hhaha.
[19:23] *Woody Evans*: actually, let's just chat here for now.
[19:23] *Woody Evans*: closed channel, right?
[19:23] *Mamacita Tarantula*: OK, I'll give you honest answers on one condition, you view some of the exhibits.
[19:24] *Mamacita Tarantula*: You can let me know what you think. Try to think of your students as patrons here.
[19:24] *Woody Evans*: I will – just point me in the direction when we're done.
[19:24] *Mamacita Tarantula*: OK, you're facing in the right direction.
[19:24] *Mamacita Tarantula*: Stand up and walk forward. You can follow me if you like.
[19:25] *Woody Evans*: And,, before we go farther – I'm using all of this for the book I mentioned. I'll alter screen names.
[19:25] *Mamacita Tarantula*: That's fine . . .
[19:25] *Mamacita Tarantula*: What's the book about?
[19:28] *Mamacita Tarantula*: This is one of the halls.
[19:31] *Woody Evans*: book is abt SL, virtual worlds
[19:31] *Woody Evans*: What's the story here?
[19:32] *Woody Evans*: WHy so much money & time. . for a ghost town?
[19:32] *Woody Evans*: A ghost town of washed up ravers?
[19:33] *Mamacita Tarantula*: People chase their youth, but listen to the music at any club, and often as not it is oldies.

[19:34] *Mamacita Tarantula*: You're home with the baby in the next room and it's too late to go out, so here is SL.

[19:34] *Mamacita Tarantula*: Not a bad deal at all when you think aboaut it.

[19:34] *Mamacita Tarantula*: Of course it gives a pretty good picture of the potential user demographic.

[19:34] *Mamacita Tarantula*: By the way where do you work?

[19:34] *Mamacita Tarantula*: I'm at [a large college near the East Coast of the United States].

[19:35] *Mamacita Tarantula*: OK our demographic is nearly all white, and nearly all people who are at least 30.

[19:35] *Mamacita Tarantula*: Average age in SL is said to be 35.

[19:35] *Mamacita Tarantula*: The music is a clue to the racial makeup.

[19:36] *Mamacita Tarantula*: You almost never find a club playing motown or R&B.

[19:36] *Woody Evans*: This is interesting.

[19:37] *Mamacita Tarantula*: I'm caucasian in real life, but I had an African American supervisor on my last job and I have African American colleagues on this job.

[19:37] *Mamacita Tarantula*: I can give you the rest of what I think of this place via email . . . .

[19:37] *Woody Evans*: You never lived in Mississippi did you?

[19:38] *Mamacita Tarantula*: No . . . . I lived in [near the Gulf of Mexico the United States]. Does that qualify?

[19:38] *Woody Evans*: I'm from MS . . anyway. this is great info. you have an interestin perspective on this. I can relate to the 'baby in the next room' stuff . . .

[19:39] *Mamacita Tarantula*: Now if this is your demogarphic, you can serve them.

[19:39] *Woody Evans*: I guess this is like Facebookk – I mean tthat it fills some of the same needs for some of the same demographics. .?

[19:39] *Mamacita Tarantula*: The other problem with SL and it's taken me a while to figure it out, is that it is more or less precapitalist.

[19:39] *Woody Evans*: Huh?

[19:39] *Mamacita Tarantula*: OK, there is money here, but no regulation and no small claim's court and zero consumer protection.

[19:40] *Mamacita Tarantula*: You make friends by doing business.

[19:40] *Woody Evans*: Is that a libertarian economic model?

[19:40] *Mamacita Tarantula*: It's not something I've ever had any experience with.

[19:40] *Woody Evans*: Why the hell do you stick with this place when you can see throught it?
[19:41] *Mamacita Tarantula*: Because I can't build a competitor.
[19:42] *Mamacita Tarantula*: What you have to realize about *Second Life* is that there is no oversight of anything, no accountabilityl.
[19:42] *Mamacita Tarantula*: If you have the money fine . . . . If you steal, you are going to get away with it in the short term.
[19:42] *Mamacita Tarantula*: In a Libertarian society there would still be a small claim's court. Ripping people off is fraud.
[19:46] Drag items from inventory here

[2010/09/27 20:16] *Woody Evans*: nobody here wants to bring me a whisky.
[2010/09/27 20:16] *Profile Greeter*: barbie Frostbite's face is up in lights!
[2010/09/27 20:16] *Fake Tina Fey Fall*: well shame on them.
[2010/09/27 20:16] *Profile Greeter*: Willa Beresford's face is up in lights!
[2010/09/27 20:17] *Mickey Rourke Bigboar*: great tunes DJ
[2010/09/27 20:17] *Woody Evans*: So. I really REALL don't get sl 'libraries'.
[2010/09/27 20:17] *Woody Evans*: Just doesn't compute . . .
[2010/09/27 20:17] *Profile Greeter*: barbie Frostbite's face is up in lights!
[2010/09/27 20:17] *Fake Tina Fey Fall*: yeah. I know.
[2010/09/27 20:17] *Fake Tina Fey Fall*: that is what I was seeing
[2010/09/27 20:17] *Celestial Orb Exxploder-G*: Come on! Feed me some lindens! Let's PLAY!
[2010/09/27 20:18] *Rickh4r77 Weirsider*: what r u seeing tina. .
[2010/09/27 20:18] *Mickey Rourke Bigboar*: brb
[2010/09/27 20:18] *Fake Tina Fey Fall*: hmmm. well I see lots of stuff
[2010/09/27 20:18] *Rickh4r77 Weirsider*: oh like what . . .
[2010/09/27 20:19] *Skyler White666*: HB
[2010/09/27 20:19] *Skyler White666*: Partyyyyy . . . . Dance . . . . Enjoy . . . . . .
[2010/09/27 20:19] *Skyler White666*: *******Where The Music's Hot *****
[2010/09/27 20:19] *Skyler White666*: ****** The Girl's Are Hotter *******
[2010/09/27 20:19] *Skyler White666*: *******Club ****** XxesS***** Rocks****
[2010/09/27 20:19] *Celestial Orb Exxploder-G*: Come on! Feed me some lindens! Let's PLAY!
[2010/09/27 20:19] *Fake Tina Fey Fall*: I see you

[2010/09/27 20:19] *Fake Tina Fey Fall*: lol and I see a purple woody
[2010/09/27 20:19] *Rickh4r77 Weirsider*: hahahaha . . . .
[2010/09/27 20:19] *Woody Evans*: Tina, I'm outtie – nice to meet you, but these robot chicks ain't doint it for me. Off for some real whisky in Real bloody Real Life. See you in here again sometime.
[2010/09/27 20:20] *Rickh4r77 Weirsider*: well im a square head . . . hahahahahah
[2010/09/27 20:20] Teleport completed from Sunset Creek (190,60,1501)

[18:22] *NoCheatin S Velde*: so i guess som things we are better
[18:22] *Fedayeen Veld3*: stop to hug me -_-
[18:22] *BailseY Wikifoo*: Anyone have any candles available?
[18:22] *JJ Kranky*: california can sink in the fucking ocean for all i care
[18:22] *NoCheatin S Velde*: some things you guys are better
[18:22] *Fedayeen Veld3*: hugging*
[18:22] *HighExplosives Heart*: ok but i will keep the memory of this forever
[18:22] *Kraken Lament*: look change time
[18:22] *BailseY Wikifoo*: Cuba's better than California anyways
[18:22] *Kraken Lament*: k
[18:22] *Kraken Lament*: done
[18:22] *Fedayeen Veld3*: -_-
[18:22] *Harlow Moontop*: now ur different too
[18:22] *HighExplosives Heart*: i will remember it in the last beat of my heart
[18:22] *Kraken Lament*: yessss
[18:22] *NoCheatin S Velde*: c'mon california have energy to them and to sale
[18:23] *NoCheatin S Velde*: and is that what we dont have
[18:23] *Fedayeen Veld3*: shut up and unstuck yourself
[18:23] *Nichola Thresharham*: touch it!
[18:23] *NoCheatin S Velde*: we need to buy
[18:23] *Fedayeen Veld3*: ah good :D
[18:23] *Kraken Lament*: I sold california to the rogue monkeys of indonesia. their ship wll be landing tomorrow morning.
[18:23] Teleport completed from Waterhead (34,74,25)
[18:27] *Woody Evans*: Is anyone here?
[18:29] *Ferrari Chassis FP*: You are not the owner of this vehicle . . .
[18:29] *Ferrari Chassis FP*: You are not the owner of this vehicle . . .
[18:30] *Illumination Library*: Welcome to the Illumination Library of Info Island International. Please enjoy your stay and do not forget to landmark us !

[18:30] Teleport completed from Info Island International (175, 157,72)
[18:30] *JJ Kranky*: corn and shit
[18:30] *Kraken Lament*: I think we can all understand Jason better now.
[18:30] *HighExplosives Heart*: your talk of a free world and freedom mean nothing because you are all enslaved to capitalism
[18:31] *HighExplosives Heart*: money
[18:31] *HighExplosives Heart*: greed
[18:31] Teleport completed from Waterhead (36,76,26)
[18:37] (*Unnamed*)(*Unnamed*): Hi, Woody!
[18:48] *Woody Evans*: Hi
[18:48] *Salamandress Pleides*: Hi
[18:48] *Woody Evans*: May I help you find anything tonight?
[18:49] *Salamandress Pleides*: I hope so. My question involves my Mac laptop and why all of a sudden I can't access SL. I'm using my husband's big Mac :)
[18:50] *Woody Evans*: Hmm
[18:50] *Woody Evans*: Does it give you any error messages?
[18:51] *Salamandress Pleides*: Last night I got a message that the braodband wasn't connected. We use wireless.
[18:51] *Salamandress Pleides*: My typing motion isn't working . . .
[18:52] *Salamandress Pleides*: I can't get the message to come back up. My little timer just sits and spins the control alt delete says it's not responding
[18:52] *Woody Evans*: Fair warning: I'm not a computer expert, or a Mac guy – I'm just a librarian.
[18:52] *Woody Evans*: But what I'd do is Uninstall *Second Life*
[18:52] *Woody Evans*: then reinstall it.
[18:53] *Salamandress Pleides*: Will I lose myself :)
[18:53] *Woody Evans*: Your current session will end.,,
[18:53] *Woody Evans*: but you're avatar will survive because
[18:53] *Salamandress Pleides*: But me myself and my inverntory will be OK?
[18:53] *Woody Evans*: you have an account
[18:53] *Woody Evans*: Yes, all that stuff is on Lindens servers somewhere.
[18:54] *Salamandress Pleides*: maybe in third life heheeh
[18:54] *Woody Evans*: Right! Haha
[18:54] *Woody Evans*: Hey,
[18:54] *Woody Evans*: what do you do in SL?
[18:54] *Salamandress Pleides*: I'm a librarian my self and came directly to CVL for help. I know [one of the librarians here].

[18:54] *Woody Evans*: I don't come here often. I'm here to scc whats' up at the 'library' b/c I'm a librarian
[18:54] *Woody Evans*: Oh.
[18:55] *Woody Evans*: Do you think this Virtual Library is a good thing?
[18:55] *Woody Evans*: Does it work?
[18:55] *Woody Evans*: What's it for?
[18:55] *Woody Evans*: etc.
[18:56] *Salamandress Pleides*: I've been here a few times and the librarians at the desk have always been helpful. Are you a volunteer here?
[18:57] *Woody Evans*: No
[18:57] *Woody Evans*: I'm writing a book about this place.
[18:57] *Woody Evans*: sort of.
[18:57] *Salamandress Pleides*: oh
[18:58] *Woody Evans*: I just dropped in to see what was shaking.
[18:58] *Woody Evans*: Sit on a wall.
[18:58] *Woody Evans*: etc.
[18:58] *Woody Evans*: It's dead here . . . you see folsk in here much?
[18:58] *Salamandress Pleides*: I know to work at the Refence desk in CVL you have to shadow an established CVL librarian volunteer.
[18:59] *Woody Evans*: Ha!
[18:59] *Woody Evans*: that might be fun, actually.
[18:59] *Woody Evans*: Well, I've never shadowed CVL whatsits, and if your Mac issue turns out all right, I think we'll be doing all right.
[19:00] *Woody Evans*: If not . . . well.
[19:01] *Salamandress Pleides*: well, I think I'll make sure from a recognized CVL REF librarian whether or not to do as you say. You could be anyone. adios
[19:02] *Woody Evans*: hahaha
[19:02] *Woody Evans*: I am anyone.
[19:02] *Woody Evans*: Bye.
[19:03] *Catalina the Library Cat* whispers: Sorry, I don't know you
[19:03] *Catalina the Library Cat* whispers: Sorry, I don't know you
[19:03] *Woody Evans*: What the fu . . . ?!
[19:03] *Woody Evans*: Oh.
[19:03] *Woody Evans*: You're a cat.
[19:03] *Woody Evans*: Thought you were a chupacabra for a second.
[19:04] *Woody Evans*: Don't come any closer and we'll be just fine.
[19:04] (*Unnamed*)(*Unnamed*) Hi, Woody!
[19:04] *Woody Evans*: Is this the stool chatting me up?
[19:07] *Woody Evans*: Hi Balboa
[19:07] *Balboa Bibliotheque*: Hi Woody

[19:08] *Balboa Bibliotheque*: How's it going?
[19:08] *Woody Evans*: Good.
[19:08] *Woody Evans*: You the usual here?
[19:08] *Woody Evans*: Your shift?
[19:08] *Balboa Bibliotheque*: yeah . . . .
[19:08] *Balboa Bibliotheque*: Tuesdays, 7–9
[19:08] *Woody Evans*: Here.
[19:08] *Woody Evans*: Have a seat.
[19:08] *Balboa Bibliotheque*: unfortunately our son is visiting from Washington DC so I may not be here long tonight
[19:08] *Balboa Bibliotheque*: nah . . . I like to stand . . .
[19:09] *Woody Evans*: Just got my toddeler down no tlong ago
[19:09] *Balboa Bibliotheque*: lol . . . if I sit I'll fall asleep
[19:09] *Woody Evans*: So. .
[19:09] *Balboa Bibliotheque*: :) and our grandson just felll asleep too
[19:09] *Woody Evans*: I'm writing a book about SL sorto of.
[19:09] *Balboa Bibliotheque*: cool
[19:09] *Woody Evans*: And I just don't get this place.
[19:09] *Woody Evans*: particularly the 'libraries' . . .
[19:09] *Balboa Bibliotheque*: this place meaning the library?
[19:09] *Balboa Bibliotheque*: why's that?
[19:09] *Woody Evans*: Do you get ref work ?
[19:10] *Woody Evans*: Well,, do folks come and ask questions?
[19:10] *Balboa Bibliotheque*: some nights I might get 20 people . . . some nights 1–2
[19:10] *Balboa Bibliotheque*: ohhhh. . the questions!
[19:10] *Balboa Bibliotheque*: noda
[19:10] *Balboa Bibliotheque*: nods
[19:10] *Balboa Bibliotheque*: Think about it
[19:10] *Balboa Bibliotheque*: if you work at a publc or community library
[19:10] *Balboa Bibliotheque*: and folks come in . . . not just students
[19:11] *Balboa Bibliotheque*: many of them are going to have questions about . . . the community
[19:11] *Balboa Bibliotheque*: that's what happens here
[19:11] *Balboa Bibliotheque*: most of the questions have to do with SL
[19:11] *Balboa Bibliotheque*: Hi Maynard
[19:11] *Balboa Bibliotheque*: woops . . . he moved too fast :)
[19:12] *Woody Evans*: Hm
[19:12] *Balboa Bibliotheque*: 'How do I change my shape' 'Where can I find a good cowboy hat' etc
[19:12] *Woody Evans*: that's an intersting point.

[19:12] *Balboa Bibliotheque*: I think the number is 85–90 percent of the ref questions we get
[19:12] *Woody Evans*: So why do YOU do it?
[19:12] *Balboa Bibliotheque: Second Life*
[19:12] *Woody Evans*: Why invest in this world, this community, these people?
[19:13] *Balboa Bibliotheque*: I've been a librarian for 33 years. . I love my job. I came into SL wondering how it might expand how I approach being a librarian . . . and got hooked
[19:13] *Balboa Bibliotheque*: why not?
[19:13] *Balboa Bibliotheque*: I spend one evening a week here
[19:13] *Balboa Bibliotheque*: that's it
[19:13] *Balboa Bibliotheque*: not much to ask
[19:13] *Balboa Bibliotheque*: and I enjoy meeting these people . . . from all over th eworld. I'm from Kansas in RL
[19:14] *Balboa Bibliotheque*: it's an amazing 'jump' to stand here
[19:14] *Balboa Bibliotheque*: and helps someone from Japan
[19:14] *Balboa Bibliotheque*: *help
[19:15] *Balboa Bibliotheque*: and of course it keeps me off the street stealing hubcaps too
[19:15] *Woody Evans*: :)
[19:15] *Woody Evans*: I guess neither one of us is in the pool hall rightnow. .
[19:16] *Woody Evans*: Well. thansk for sharing that, Balboa.
[19:16] *Balboa Bibliotheque*: sure
[19:16] *Woody Evans*: Hadn't heard that angle before.
[19:16] *Woody Evans*: I'm pretty hard on SL, usually.
[19:16] *Balboa Bibliotheque*: really? wow . . . I
[19:16] *Balboa Bibliotheque*: when I got in here 4 years ago
[19:17] *Balboa Bibliotheque*: I never chatted . . . . explored anything beyond email and OCLC cataloging
[19:17] *Balboa Bibliotheque*: I got in here and met folks. . other librarians . . . started talking to them outside SL
[19:17] *Balboa Bibliotheque*: met them at conferences
[19:17] *Balboa Bibliotheque*: and my world. . my professional world changed
[19:18] *Woody Evans*: Can I ask you something?
[19:18] *Balboa Bibliotheque*: sure
[19:18] *Woody Evans*: Given that some librarians do this on the job, or as part of their job,,
[19:18] *Woody Evans*: how does SL help a real life patron?
[19:18] *Woody Evans*: you know?

[19:19] *Woody Evans*: Does this world have any track back to Real World service?

[19:20] *Balboa Bibliotheque*: good question . . . . I can think of individual cases where yes, it does . . . But I suppose folks couls argue that that is minor stuf

[19:20] *Balboa Bibliotheque*: we have a library here in SL. . 'The STatte LIbrary of Kansas Vittual Branch

[19:20] *Balboa Bibliotheque*: I can give you the LM if you'd like

[19:21] *Balboa Bibliotheque*: we stuff that parcel full of info on Kansas, Kansas libraries, services to kansans in education, libraries, government, charities, etc

[19:21] *Woody Evans*: Actually been over there

[19:21] *Balboa Bibliotheque*: and I have various ways for folks to contact me

[19:21] *Balboa Bibliotheque*: maybe 1–5 times a month I get emails or IMs . . . 'Wow. . I didn't know I could do this in Kansas. . or this was available' SO on a small level there

[19:21] *Balboa Bibliotheque*: yes

[19:22] *Balboa Bibliotheque*: for those folks who probably did a serach for 'kansas' in the SL search engine it was helpful in RL

[19:22] *Balboa Bibliotheque*: on another level

[19:22] *Balboa Bibliotheque*: last night we had 3 Kansas libraryu directors up on Imnfo Island

[19:22] *Balboa Bibliotheque*: doing a panel on 'book challenges'

[19:23] *Balboa Bibliotheque*: the sim was nearly full

[19:23] *Balboa Bibliotheque*: an entire class from a graduate library school program was present . . . and these three directors gave a very practical presentation

[19:23] *Balboa Bibliotheque*: on what its like to have a book challenged

[19:23] *Balboa Bibliotheque*: and the questions were great

[19:23] *Balboa Bibliotheque*: two things right there

[19:24] *Woody Evans*: I see.

[19:24] *Woody Evans*: So it's contact for folks already here,, but also meeting/dialog with colleagues. .

[19:24] *Balboa Bibliotheque*: there's also the graphics part of it too

[19:25] *Balboa Bibliotheque*: the seemingly 3 D presentation

[19:25] *Balboa Bibliotheque*: I had a friend try to explain the 4th dimension to me one night

[19:25] *Balboa Bibliotheque*: I was totaly lost

[19:25] *Balboa Bibliotheque*: and he got this idea and whipped up this . . . just a sec

[19:28] *Balboa Bibliotheque*: he set out a hypercube
[19:28] *Balboa Bibliotheque*: and continued his discussion
[19:28] *Balboa Bibliotheque*: while I walked around it
[19:28] *Balboa Bibliotheque*: and the next day I went to th elibrary and read some more and looked at seom 2D pics
[19:28] *Balboa Bibliotheque*: 2 D
[19:29] *Balboa Bibliotheque*: and I got it
[19:29] *Balboa Bibliotheque*: sorta :)
[19:29] *Balboa Bibliotheque*: that 3 D vision on my screen helped
[19:29] *Woody Evans*: Haha That's great. Object lesson, huh?
[19:29] *Balboa Bibliotheque*: nods
[19:29] *Woody Evans*: Is this thing a 'tesseract'?
[19:29] *Woody Evans*: funky.
[19:30] *Balboa Bibliotheque*: and gues what . . . the guy who explained all this to me . . . a librarian?. . no a teacher. . no
[19:30] *Balboa Bibliotheque*: a security guard in RL :) another important point about libraries in virtual reality and in RL
[19:30] *Balboa Bibliotheque*: we need lots of talented people
[19:30] *Balboa Bibliotheque*: not just degreed libraraians
[19:30] *Balboa Bibliotheque*: LOL. . sorry. . my soap box
[19:30] *Woody Evans*: Yes. agree there
[19:31] *Balboa Bibliotheque*: I met that guy in SL
[19:31] *Balboa Bibliotheque*: he lives in Canada
[19:31] *Balboa Bibliotheque*: still friends
[19:31] *Woody Evans*: Good to talk to you Balboa.
[19:32] *Balboa Bibliotheque*: you too
[19:32] *Woody Evans*: Hope to see you here again sometime
[19:32] *Balboa Bibliotheque*: have a good one :)
[19:32] *Balboa Bibliotheque*: hope so too
[19:32] *Woody Evans*: :)
[19:32] *Balboa Bibliotheque*: later
[19:32] Teleport completed from Info Island International (116,232,70)
[19:32] *Triple-3skank Korobase*: oops you wife
[19:33] *JJ Kranky*: you have my sincerest thanks . . . ive been out of the loop
[19:33] *Triple-3skank Korobase*: no you are in the loop
[19:36] *Jerry J*: Lets do the fork in the garbage disposal!
[19:36] *Jerry J*: DING DING DING DING DING DING DING DING DING!
[19:37] *Willow Morales*: lol that ones new!
[19:37] *Jerry J*: is it?

[19:38] *Mavado Geistly*: ~@@@ Ayy wAssUp mY nIgG @@@~
[19:38] *Mavado Geistly*: fem boys
[19:40] *JJ Kranky*: you caped faggot
[19:42] *Triple-3skank Korobase*: omg fbi is surrounding my house and 2 black helocopters
[19:43] *Triple-3skank Korobase*: 'we have your chats on emerald'
[19:43] *Kraken Lament*: RUN, Triple-3skank.
[19:43] *Triple-3skank Korobase*: they shout
[19:43] *Triple-3skank Korobase*: no it's ok
[19:43] *Triple-3skank Korobase*: I won't give in
[19:45] *Triple-3skank Korobase*: lol
[19:45] *Mavado Geistly*: lol
[19:45] *Shannon Swiftwing*: what happened
[19:45] *Trillian Arendt*: You sound bitter, Mavado.
[19:45] *Trillian Arendt*: Have you accidentally cybered a guy?
[19:46] *Mavado Geistly*: how
[19:46] *Mavado Geistly*: its the truth aint it
[19:46] *Fina Darwinian*: bah, bad joints
[19:46] *Fina Darwinian*: and lazyness i guess
[19:46] *HighExplosives Heart*: what are you busy with?
[19:46] *Jaxx Cat Clawson*: more like watch where u sit.
[19:46] *Mavado Geistly*: u think ill call a dude a women
[19:46] *Mavado Geistly*: you got me fucked up
[19:46] *Shannon Swiftwing*: lol
[19:46] *Shannon Swiftwing*: i love it, but not happy with most of the pet owners
[19:46] *Trillian Arendt*: Who said anything about that?
[19:46] *Jaxx Cat Clawson*: was busy with a phone call
[19:46] *Fina Darwinian*: yeah
[19:46] *Mavado Geistly*: you
[19:46] *Trillian Arendt*: Point is, there are a LOT of women in SL.
[19:46] *Fina Darwinian*: :\
[19:47] *HighExplosives Heart*: so you say you dont do the slex thing
[19:47] *Fina Darwinian*: its crazy, i can remember just about ever dog i used to groom.
[19:47] *HighExplosives Heart*: ok
[19:47] *HighExplosives Heart*: but
[19:47] *HighExplosives Heart*: you are partnered
[19:47] *Fina Darwinian*: every*
[19:47] *Nympho Wilddogg*: Nympho Wilddogg stares at Trilli's adams apple.

[19:47] *Jaxx Cat Clawson*: yes. i am
[19:47] *Shannon Swiftwing*: in the summer we have alot of maggot dogs
[19:47] *HighExplosives Heart*: ok so it is a no-sex kind of deal?
[19:48] *Jaxx Cat Clawson*: mhm. .partnered my best friend
[19:48] *HighExplosives Heart*: ohhhh
[19:48] *HighExplosives Heart*: well thats nice
[19:48] *Fina Darwinian*: oh man. :(i could punch those owners in the face. and stuff some maggots in their ears.
[19:48] *Fina Darwinian*: muahahahahahahaha
[19:48] *HighExplosives Heart*: youd think it would keep guys away
[19:48] *Naughty Nicely Tillman*: Anyone may set amanda Ansia's title on /59
[19:48] *Jaxx Cat Clawson*: i know it doesnt.
[19:48] *Shannon Swiftwing*: i know
[19:48] *Fina Darwinian*: :(
[19:48] *Naughty Nicely Tillman: HighExplosives Heart* has given amanda Ansia a new title.
[19:49] *HighExplosives Heart*: lol
[19:49] *Fina Darwinian*: what is you fav dog to groom?
[19:49] *Fina Darwinian*: your*
[19:49] *HighExplosives Heart*: i dont do sl sex either
[19:50] *Ex Machina Chocolate Flava*: I do it's so hawt
[19:50] *Ex Machina Chocolate Flava*: jk
[19:50] *HighExplosives Heart*: i dont have the attention span to last for any further than /me unzips
[19:50] *Jaxx Cat Clawson*: lol.
[19:50] *HighExplosives Heart*: ok Flava
[19:50] *Ex Machina Chocolate Flava*: sup bro
[19:50] *Ex Machina Chocolate Flava*: are you like a nuke
[19:50] *Ex Machina Chocolate Flava*: explosive
[19:50] *HighExplosives Heart*: how do you do that stuff?
[19:50] *Ex Machina Chocolate Flava*: Do what
[19:51] *HighExplosives Heart*: how do you have sl sex?
[19:51] *Ex Machina Chocolate Flava*: idk easy peasy
[19:51] *Ex Machina Chocolate Flava*: sit on pose balls
[19:51] *Ex Machina Chocolate Flava*: right click, sit
[19:51] *Ex Machina Chocolate Flava*: shizam
[19:51] *HighExplosives Heart*: do you masturbate in rl?
[19:51] *Ex Machina Chocolate Flava*: uhm I do the SL sex
[19:51] *Ex Machina Chocolate Flava*: I dont do*
[19:51] *Ex Machina Chocolate Flava*: lol

[19:51] *HighExplosives Heart*: wait but you said you did
[19:51] *HighExplosives Heart*: so now when i ask if you masturbate
[19:52] *Nikky Arendt*: ok back
[19:52] *Ex Machina Chocolate Flava*: I also said 'jk'
[19:52] *HighExplosives Heart*: you escape the topic
[19:52] *HighExplosives Heart*: so you masturbate
[19:52] *Trillian Arendt*: Welcome back.
[19:52] *HighExplosives Heart*: ok
[19:52] *HighExplosives Heart*: i see
[19:52] *Nikky Arendt*: thx
[19:52] *Ex Machina Chocolate Flava*: But yeah, if I was going to get it on in SL, I guess I would masturbate.
[19:52] *HighExplosives Heart*: nothing to be ashamed of i guess
[19:52] *Ex Machina Chocolate Flava*: Masturbate to some hot pixels
[19:52] *HighExplosives Heart*: how do you type what you do while you masturbate?
[19:52] *Ex Machina Chocolate Flava*: One hand
[19:52] *HighExplosives Heart*: you get off on pixels?
[19:52] *Ex Machina Chocolate Flava*: ;]
[19:53] *Ex Machina Chocolate Flava*: All the time I love pixels, they're hot
[19:53] *HighExplosives Heart*: ok sorry im trolling i shoudn't . . .
[19:53] *Ex Machina Chocolate Flava*: especially when they're arranged to form a nice set of tits
[19:53] *HighExplosives Heart*: old habit
[19:53] *Ex Machina Chocolate Flava*: Yeah, you're not trolling.
[19:53] *Ex Machina Chocolate Flava*: lol
[19:53] *Jaxx Cat Clawson*: lol.
[19:53] *HighExplosives Heart*: ok dont push it
[19:53] *Ex Machina Chocolate Flava*: Push what? Your buttons?
[19:53] *HighExplosives Heart*: you just admited to getting off on pixels
[19:54] *HighExplosives Heart*: i could take that further
[19:54] *Ex Machina Chocolate Flava*: Take it further.
[19:54] *HighExplosives Heart*: not in the modd
[19:54] *HighExplosives Heart*: mood
[19:54] *Trillian Arendt*: Lol.
[19:54] *Ex Machina Chocolate Flava*: Lame, are you on your period.
[19:54] *Trillian Arendt*: Cop out.
[19:54] *Nympho Wilddogg*: I am.
[19:54] *Ex Machina Chocolate Flava*: Great :)

[19:54] *HighExplosives Heart*: oh god it has been beaten to death to troll somebody over pixel sex

[19:55] *Trillian Arendt*: Clearly you're an expert at it.

[19:55] *Ex Machina Chocolate Flava*: Mr. Nuclear Weapon High Explosive guy

[19:55] *Ex Machina Chocolate Flava*: He's got other high explosives ;]

[19:55] *Ex Machina Chocolate Flava*: Probably when he's jackin' it to pixels.

[19:56] *Ex Machina Chocolate Flava*: Ain't that right?

[19:56] *Jaxx Cat Clawson*: :>

[19:56] *Ex Machina Chocolate Flava*: Oh, sorry, I'm trolling, bad habbit.

[19:56] *Nikky Arendt*: so fina had a baby 'she named it Trilli

[19:56] *HighExplosives Heart*: k

[19:56] *Trillian Arendt*: Just like we will name ours.

[19:56] *Nikky Arendt*: for real though fina had a baby

[19:56] *Nikky Arendt*: tell her congrats!

[19:56] *Trillian Arendt*: That's awesome! Congratulations.

[19:56] *HighExplosives Heart*: jax what do you do in sl?

[19:57] *Trillian Arendt*: How long has it been now?

[19:57] *Nikky Arendt*: she had a baby and he's 8 months old now – so it's been a long time

[19:57] *Ex Machina Chocolate Flava*: Are you trying to get with JaX so you can pixel sex her later?

[19:57] *Jaxx Cat Clawson*: build, script, dj, manage a club.

[19:57] *Trillian Arendt*: Nice. (:

[19:57] *Jaxx Cat Clawson*: lol. Flava its not gonna work:/

[19:57] *HighExplosives Heart*: did you build any of your stuff?

[19:57] *Ex Machina Chocolate Flava*: Lol, I know, but he thinks it is, since he's still trying.

[19:57] *Nikky Arendt*: he's precious I saw pics

[19:57] *Jaxx Cat Clawson*: nope not what im wearing today.

[19:58] *HighExplosives Heart*: what kind of stuff did you build?

[19:58] *Trillian Arendt*: Well . . . I hate babies! But whatever.

[19:58] Pincer Panhandler: 'I'm a DJ in *Second Life*.' 'HAHAHAHA HAHA.'

[19:58] *Trillian Arendt*: That's still awesome.

[19:58] *Jaxx Cat Clawson*: radom crap . . . jewelry, skyboxes, avi's

[19:58] *Nikky Arendt*: pls no one hates babies

[19:58] *HighExplosives Heart*: well if no weapons it isnt fun

[19:58] *Nikky Arendt*: I love babies but only if I get to hold them and give them back to their mothers
[19:58] *HighExplosives Heart*: you should make some
[19:58] *Jaxx Cat Clawson*: i have
[19:59] *HighExplosives Heart*: are they any good?
[19:59] *Jaxx Cat Clawson*: if u like chickens pushing and following u, then yes. they are good
[19:59] *Jaxx Cat Clawson*: hello [shyrus] :)
[20:00] *Jaxx Cat Clawson*: how u doin?
[20:00] *Jaxx Cat Clawson*: doing good. :)
[20:00] *Jaxx Cat Clawson*: ;o
[20:00] *Jaxx Cat Clawson*: what kind?
[20:00] *Jaxx Cat Clawson*: ;o
[20:00] *Jaxx Cat Clawson*: flavor?
[20:00] *Jaxx Cat Clawson*: yum
[20:01] *Trillian Arendt*: I have to eat my fortune cookie now. Let's see if it says anything about us.
[20:01] *Jaxx Cat Clawson*: i had phish food.
[20:01] *Jaxx Cat Clawson*: its alright.
[20:01] *Jaxx Cat Clawson*: yes.
[20:01] *Jaxx Cat Clawson*: :)
[20:01] *Trillian Arendt*: 'You will soon receive an unusual gift'

The chatting in Waterhead goes on like this. And on, and on. These are our potential patrons over at community college libraries, and the Community Virtual Library, and university libraries. These are our potential clients as private researchers and information professionals.

Appendix II: TOS

In an age of Digital Rights Management, licensing of music and books, and the leveraging of privacy (and identity) by corporate interests, legal language is loaded and revealing. DRM, as it is shortened, suggests that 'rights' are something than can be, and perhaps should be, *managed*. But managed by whom, or by what entities? As a user enters a virtual world, she needs to be mightily mindful of the terms by which she passes through the gates.

What follows is a record of the legalese (as of mid-to-late 2010) presented to folks entering two virtual worlds: *Runescape* and *Second Life*. These two worlds were selected because they represent very different kinds of experiences. As described in great detail above, *Runescape* is kind of juvenile, somewhat clunky (and endearing in its honest clunkiness), and very unapologetically genre-oriented. *Second Life* is, on the other hand, mature (adult-oriented), slick (though often disappointing when its slickness fails), and more-or-less non-genre in structure (though it is host to countless genres and subgenres). A static record of the Terms of Service (in print, and in a book about libraries, media, and information service) of these two distinct and unalike worlds in late 2010 offers important contrasts and – most importantly – much similarity.

Terms of Service, legal notices, DRM consents, and privacy policies all change over time – and sometimes in quite short order. So the words below will shift on the sites that host them as needs, social and legal atmospheres, and corporate prerogatives demand it. But, captured statically here (for a little while at least) you may study, dig into, and parse the end-user agreements that are all too often whipped before us in a flash, leaving too little time for sustained and careful consideration.

Here's your chance to read and think with a book in hand – how will these Terms of Service affect you, your peers, and your organization, as you move a foot into a virtual world? They are offered without comment.

So take some time to figure on the issue. Reckon all conceivable angles. Act with care and deliberateness.

Consider yourself, here on out, reasonably informed.

Second Life's Terms of Service

Last updated: March 31, 2010
Effective date: April 30, 2010

Welcome to *Second Life*! This agreement (this 'Agreement' or the 'Terms of Service') describes the terms on which Linden Research, Inc. ('Linden Lab') offers you access to *Second Life*. '*Second Life*' or the 'Service' means the multi-user online service offered by Linden Lab, including its Websites, Servers, Linden Software, Linden Inworld Content, and User Content (as those terms are defined in this Agreement). This offer is conditioned on your agreement to all of the terms and conditions contained in the Terms of Service, including the policies and terms linked to or otherwise referenced in this Agreement.

By using *Second Life*, you agree to and accept these Terms of Service. If you do not so agree, you should decline this Agreement, in which case you are prohibited from accessing or using *Second Life*.

Table of contents

This Agreement includes both the terms above and the following 14 sections, which you may jump to directly by selecting the appropriate link below. The headings and subheadings are for your convenience only – you are responsible for reviewing all sections, defined terms and related links in their entirety to ensure you fully understand this Agreement.

The Service currently includes a component called 'Currency Exchange' or 'LindeX™,' which refers to an aspect of the Service through which Linden Lab administers transactions among users for the purchase and sale of the licensed right to use Currency. Notwithstanding any other language or context to the contrary, as used in this Agreement and throughout the Service in the context of Currency transfer:

(a) the term 'sell' means 'to transfer for consideration to another user the licensed right to use Currency in accordance with the Terms of Service,'

(b) the term 'buy' means 'to receive for consideration from another user the licensed right to use Currency in accordance with the Terms of Service,'

(c) the terms 'buyer,' 'seller', 'sale' and 'purchase' and similar terms have corresponding meanings to the root terms 'buy' and 'sell,'

(d) 'sell order' and similar terms mean a request from a user to Linden Lab to list Currency for sale on the Currency Exchange at a requested sale price, and

(e) 'buy order' and similar terms mean a request from a user for Linden Lab to match open sale listings with a requested purchase price and facilitate completion of the sale of Currency.

1. Changes to this agreement

This Agreement may be changed by Linden Lab effective immediately by notifying you as provided in Section 13.4 below; provided that Material Changes will become effective thirty (30) days after such notification. By continuing to access or use *Second Life* after the effective date of any such change, you agree to be bound by the modified Terms of Service. A 'Material Change' is a change to this Agreement that reduces your contractual rights or increases your responsibilities under this Agreement in a significant manner.

Return to top

2. *Eligibility to use* Second Life

2.1 *Age Requirements for* Second Life

By accepting this Agreement in connection with an Account (other than for Teen *Second Life*), you represent that you are at least 18 years of age, or the legal age of majority where you reside if that jurisdiction has an older age of majority, and you have the legal authority to enter into this Agreement.

2.2 Age Requirements for Teen *Second Life*

By accepting this Agreement in connection with an Account for use in Teen *Second Life*, you represent that:

(i) you are at least 13 years of age and less than 18 years of age;

(ii) you will not continue to use Teen *Second Life* after you turn 18;

(iii) your parent or legal guardian has consented to your having an Account in Teen *Second Life*, participating in the Service, and providing your personal information in connection with the Service; and

(iv) your parent or legal guardian has read and accepted this Agreement on your behalf. If you are under 13 years of age, then please do not use Teen *Second Life*. There are lots of other great virtual world services for you. Talk to your parents about which services are appropriate for you.

2.3 Age Verification for Adult Only *Second Life*

In order to access *Second Life* regions or listings designated as 'Adult Only' Content (which Content may be explicitly sexual, intensely violent or otherwise designated as Adult under our Maturity Ratings ('Adult Only Content'), you affirm that you are at least 18 years of age, or the age of legal majority where you reside if that jurisdiction has an older age of majority. You further agree that as a condition to accessing Adult Only *Second Life*, you will submit to account verification as required by

Linden, and provide only true and accurate identification documentation to Linden or its third party service providers to verify your age. You further acknowledge that you will comply with our Maturity Ratings, and conduct any activities we have defined as Adult only within regions designated as Adult.

2.4 Requirements for Corporate Users

If you are using the Service on behalf of a company, organization or other legal entity (collectively, 'User Organization'), you represent and warrant that you are an employee of that User Organization or other person authorized to do so.

2.5 Other Eligibility Requirements for Use of *Second Life*

You may not use or register to use *Second Life*:

(i) for the duration of your suspension if you have been suspended from the Service by Linden Lab;

(ii) at any time if you have been terminated from the Service by Linden Lab; or

(iii) at any time if you are a person barred from receiving the Services under applicable law.

Return to top

3. Account registration and billing

3.1 You must establish an account to use *Second Life*, using true and accurate registration information

You must establish an Account with Linden Lab to use the Service, except for those portions of the Websites that Linden Lab allows users to access without registration. You may establish one or more additional Accounts, provided that your existing Account is in good standing and you are otherwise in full compliance with this Agreement. You may not transfer or assign your Account and its contractual rights, licenses and obligations, to any third party without the prior written consent of Linden Lab.

You agree to provide accurate, current and complete information about yourself as prompted by the registration form ('Registration Data') and to use the account management tools provided to keep your Registration Data accurate, current and complete.

You may establish an Account with Registration Data provided to Linden Lab by a third party who provides a gateway to our Service through the use of an API, in which case you may have a separate, additional account relationship with such third party. This relationship in no way modifies, lessens or alters your obligations under this Terms of Service. Access to *Second Life* through third parties may be available or discontinued at the discretion of Linden Lab. You acknowledge that Linden Lab is not liable for the acts or omissions of such third parties, which are not the partner or representative of Linden Lab or endorsed or controlled by Linden Lab.

3.2 You agree to use an Account Name in *Second Life* that is not misleading, offensive or infringing. You are responsible for activities related to your Account Name, and for keeping your password for this Account secure

You must choose an account name to identify yourself to Linden Lab staff in connection with your Account (your 'Account Name'), which will also serve as the name for your graphical representation within the Service under this Account (your 'Avatar'). You may not select as your Account Name any name that Linden Lab determines may cause deception or confusion; may violate any trademark right, copyright, or other proprietary right or mislead other users regarding your identity or affiliation; or any name that Linden Lab determines in its discretion to be vulgar, offensive, or otherwise inappropriate. Linden Lab reserves the right to delete or change any Account Name that violates this paragraph, and will have no liability regarding the use or deletion of any Account Name.

You are responsible for all activities conducted through your Account. In the event that fraud, illegality or other conduct that violates this Agreement is discovered or reported (whether by you or someone else) that is connected with your Account, we may suspend or terminate your Account (or Accounts) as described in Section 11.

At the time your Account is opened, you must select a password. You are responsible for maintaining the confidentiality of your password and are responsible for any harm resulting from your disclosure, or authorization of the disclosure of your password or from any person's use of your password to gain access to your Account or Account Name. At no time should you respond to an online request for a password other than in connection with the log-on process to the Service. Your disclosure of your password to any other person is at your own risk.

3.3 If you choose to use paid aspects of the Service, you agree to the posted pricing and billing policies on the Websites

Certain aspects of the Service, including the usage of virtual environments known as 'Virtual Land' in *Second Life*, or subscription to a 'premium account', are provided for a fee or other charge. These fees and charges are set forth on the Second Life Fee Schedule. Should you elect to use paid aspects of the Service, you agree to the pricing, payment and billing policies posted on the Websites applicable to such fees and charges, plus VAT or other taxes as applicable, including as set forth in the Second Life Billing Policy, and in the Xstreet SL Billing Policy. Linden Lab may add new services for additional fees and charges, or prospectively amend fees and charges for existing services.

You acknowledge that it is your responsibility to ensure payment in advance for all paid aspects of the Service, and to ensure that your credit or debit cards or other payment instruments accepted by Linden Lab continue to be valid and sufficient for such purposes. Linden Lab may exercise its suspension or termination rights as provided in Section 11.3 in the event of any payment delinquency.

Linden Lab does not accept returns or provide refunds of products or services purchased from Linden Lab. For disclosure purposes, the legal name under which Linden Lab does business is Linden Research, Inc. and the address from which business is conducted is 945 Battery Street, San Francisco, California 94111.

Return to top

4. Second Life *is a virtual world service*

4.1 *Second Life* is a virtual world service consisting of a multi-user environment, including software, websites and virtual spaces

'Account' means the entirety of your contractual rights and obligations under this Agreement associated with a particular Account Name you have selected for accessing the Service.

'Content' means any works of authorship, creative works, graphics, images, textures, photos, logos, sounds, music, video, audio, computer programs, applications, animations, gestures, text, objects, primitives, scripts, and interactive features.

'Intellectual Property Rights' means copyrights, trademarks, service marks, trade dress, publicity rights, database rights, patent rights, and other intellectual property rights or proprietary rights recognized by law.

'Inworld' means within the three-dimensional virtual world environment of *Second Life*.

'Linden Inworld Content' is the Content provided to you Inworld by Linden Lab under license in connection with the Service, except all User Content (as defined below), including but not limited to Content we created or licensed from third parties.

'Linden Software' is the software provided to you by Linden Lab and/or its suppliers under license in connection with the Service, including but not limited to the viewer software for accessing the *Second Life* environment (the 'Viewer'), any other communication software, whether facilitating text-based, chat-based, voice, audio or other communication, within or outside of the *Second Life* environment, and any application program interfaces for use with *Second Life* (the 'APIs').

'*Second Life*' or the 'Service' is the multi-user online service offered by Linden Lab and includes the Websites, Servers, Linden Software, Linden Inworld Content, and User Content.

'Servers' are the online environments that support the Service, including without limitation: the server computation, electronic data storage, software access, messaging and protocols that simulate the *Second Life* environment.

'User Content' means any Content that a user of the Service has uploaded, published, or submitted to or through the Servers, Websites, or other areas of the Service.

'Websites' are the websites and services available from the domain and subdomains of http://secondlife.com and http://xstreetsl.com and any related or successor domains from which Linden Lab may offer services.

4.2 *Second Life* exists only as long as and in the form that we may provide the Service, and all aspects of the Service are subject to change or elimination

Linden Lab has the right to change and/or eliminate any aspect(s), features or functionality of the Service as it sees fit at any time without notice, and Linden Lab makes no commitment, express or implied, to maintain or continue any aspect of the Service. You acknowledge that your use of the Service is subject to this risk and that you knowingly assume it and make your decisions to participate in the Service, contribute Content and spend your money accordingly.

4.3 Linden Lab is a service provider and is not responsible or liable for the Content, conduct, or services of users or third parties

You understand that Linden Lab is a service provider that enables its users to interact online and display and communicate information and Content chosen by those users, and that users likewise can alter the service environment on a real-time basis. Linden Lab does not control or endorse the Content of communications between users or users' interactions with each other or the Service.

You acknowledge that you will be exposed to various aspects of the Service involving the conduct, Content, and services of users, and that Linden Lab does not control and is not responsible or liable for the quality, safety, legality, truthfulness or accuracy of any such user conduct, User Content, or user services. You acknowledge that Linden Lab does not guarantee the accuracy of information submitted by any user of the Service, nor any identity information about any user. Your interactions with other users and your use and purchase of User Content or user services are entirely at your own risk.

You agree that Linden Lab has and may exercise the right in its sole discretion to pre-screen, refuse, or delete any Content or services from the Service or disable any user's access to the Service without notice or liability to you or any other party, including upon our belief that such user's conduct, Content, services, or use of the Service is potentially illegal, threatening, or otherwise harmful to any user or other person or in violation of our Terms of Service, Community Standards, or other policies.

The Service may contain links to or otherwise allow connections to third-party websites, servers, and online services or environments that are not owned or controlled by Linden Lab. You agree that Linden Lab is not responsible or liable for the Content, policies, or practices of any third-party websites, servers, or online services or environments. Please consult any applicable terms of use and privacy policies provided by the third party for such websites, servers, or online services or environments.

4.4 If properly notified, Linden Lab responds to complaints that User Content infringes another's intellectual property

Intellectual property infringement on the Service is a violation of this Terms of Service, and you agree not to engage in such infringement. It is our policy to respond to notices of alleged copyright infringement that comply with the Digital Millennium Copyright Act and to terminate the accounts of repeat infringers in appropriate circumstances. We operate an intellectual property complaint process for complaints that User Content infringes another's intellectual property, the details of which are available in our Intellectual Property Policy. Linden Lab reserves the right to disable, delete or terminate, without notice, any user's Content or access to the Service if that user is determined by Linden Lab to infringe or repeatedly infringe.

4.5 *Second Life* is subject to scheduled and unscheduled service interruptions and loss of server data, which you do not own and for which you will not hold us liable

Linden Lab may on occasion need to interrupt the Service with or without prior notice. You agree that Linden Lab will not be liable for any interruption of the Service (whether intentional or not), and you understand that except as may otherwise be specifically provided in Linden Lab's Billing Policy, you will not be entitled to any refunds of fees or other compensation for interruption of service.

Likewise, you agree that in the event of data loss, we will not be liable for any purported damage or harm arising therefrom. Linden Lab owns the bits and bytes of electronic data stored on its Servers, and accordingly will not be liable for any deletion, corruption or data loss that occurs in connection with the Service. Linden Lab will solely determine any disposition of the electronic data stored on its Servers and will have no obligation to reproduce, process, transfer, extract or recreate any data from its Servers. Our ownership of these bits and bytes of electronic data stored on our Servers does not limit or impair any Intellectual Property Rights you may have in your Content as set forth in Section 7.1 below.

Return to top

5. *'Linden dollars' are virtual tokens that we license*

5.1 Each Linden dollar is a virtual token representing contractual permission from Linden Lab to access features of the Service. Linden dollars are available for Purchase or distribution at Linden Lab's discretion, and are not redeemable for monetary value from Linden Lab

The Service includes a component of virtual tokens ('Linden dollars' or 'L$'), each of which constitutes a limited license permission to use features of our Service as set forth below. Linden Lab may or may not charge fees to acquire or use Linden dollars, and these fees may change at any time.

When you acquire a Linden dollar, Linden Lab hereby grants you a limited license ('Linden Dollar License') to use the Linden dollar as a virtual token to be held, bartered, traded and/or transferred in *Second Life* with other users (and/or Linden Lab), in exchange for permission to access and use Content, applications, services, and various user-created features, in accordance with these Terms of Service. The Linden Dollar License is transferable by the holder to any other user, provided that both users comply with these Terms of Service, maintain their Accounts in good standing, and are not delinquent on any Account payment requirements. Except as expressly permitted by this Agreement or otherwise expressly permitted by Linden Lab, the Linden Dollar License may not be sublicensed, encumbered, conveyed or made subject to any right of survivorship or other disposition by operation of law or otherwise, and you agree that any attempted disposition in violation of these Terms of Service is null and void. Linden Lab may revoke the Linden Dollar License at any time without notice, refund or compensation in the event that:

(i) the Linden dollar program is suspended or discontinued;

(ii) Linden Lab determines that fraud or other illegal conduct is associated with the holder's Account;

(iii) Linden Lab imposes an expiration date on usage of Linden dollars in compliance with applicable laws and regulations;

(iv) the holder's Account is terminated for violation of these Terms of Service; or

(v) the holder becomes delinquent on any of that user's Account payment requirements, ceases to maintain an active Account or terminates this Agreement.

You acknowledge that Linden dollars are not real currency or any type of financial instrument and are not redeemable for any sum of money from Linden Lab at any time. You agree that Linden Lab has the right to manage, regulate, control, and/or modify the license rights underlying such Linden dollars as it sees fit and that Linden Lab will have no liability to you based on its exercise of this right. Linden Lab makes no guarantee as to the nature, quality or value of the features of the Service that will be accessible through the use of Linden dollars, or the availability or supply of Linden dollars.

5.2 *Second Life* offers a Linden dollar exchange, called the LindeX exchange, for the trading of Linden dollars, which uses the terms 'Buy' and 'Sell' to indicate the transfer of Linden Dollar Licenses

The Service includes a component called the 'LindeX exchange' or the 'LindeX,' which refers to an aspect of the Service through which Linden Lab permits transactions in which users may exchange their Linden dollars with one another. The Service includes other, similar Linden dollar exchange sites and methods, including the Xstreet 'Currency Exchange' at xstreetsl.com, and the Service may from time to time include other, similar methods or sites on which Linden dollars may be exchanged (referred to collectively as the 'LindeX' or 'LindeX exchange'). You acknowledge that the LindeX exchange has been created to enable users of *Second Life* to enhance their experience using the Service with the ability to transfer license rights to other users of the Service, and that the terminology used is solely for the purpose of enabling this use of the Service.

Regardless of terminology used, you acknowledge that as used in this Agreement and throughout the Service in the context of Linden dollar transfers:

(a) the term 'Sell' means 'to transfer for consideration to another user their Linden dollars in accordance with the Terms of Service,'

(b) the term 'Buy' or 'Purchase' means 'to receive for consideration from another user their Linden dollars in accordance with the Terms of Service,'

(c) the terms 'Buyer,' 'Seller,' 'Sale' and 'Purchaser' and similar terms have corresponding meanings to their root terms,

(d) 'Sell Order' and similar terms mean a request from a user to Linden Lab to list Linden dollars for Sale on the LindeX exchange at a requested Sale price, and

(e) 'Buy Order' and similar terms mean a request from a user for Linden Lab to match open Sale listings with a requested Purchase price and facilitate completion of the Sale of Linden dollars.

You acknowledge that Linden Lab may deny any Sell order or Buy order individually or with respect to general volume, price or other limitations set by Linden Lab. Linden Lab may halt, suspend, discontinue, or reverse any LindeX exchange transaction (whether proposed, pending or past) in cases of actual or suspected fraud, violations of other laws or regulations, or deliberate disruptions to or interference with the Service.

5.3 There are other Linden dollar exchanges that are operated by third parties

Linden dollars are occasionally Bought and Sold on third party exchanges, which are wholly distinct from the LindeX exchange. Unless specified by Linden Lab, these exchanges have no affiliation with Linden Lab. We do not guarantee the legitimacy of the Linden dollar transfers offered on them, and we are not liable for purchases of such Linden dollars. You purchase Linden dollars from such sites at your own risk. If you Buy Linden dollars that are traced to unauthorized credit card activity or other fraudulent activity, we will recoup these Linden dollars from your Account.

Purely for informational purposes, we may list on our Websites third-party exchanges that use our 'Risk API' tool. The use of the Risk API may lessen the occurrence of fraud on those exchanges; however, in no event do we endorse, guarantee or insure your purchases from these unaffiliated exchanges.

Return to top

6. *'Virtual land' is inworld space that we license*

Virtual Land is the graphical representation of three-dimensional virtual world space. When you acquire Virtual Land, you obtain a limited license to access and use certain features of the Service associated with Virtual Land stored on our Servers. Virtual Land is available for Purchase or distribution at Linden Lab's discretion, and is not redeemable for monetary value from Linden Lab.

The Service includes a component of Inworld virtual space that is stored on our Servers and made available in the form of virtual units ('Virtual Land'). This 'Virtual Land' constitutes a limited license to access and use certain features of our Service as set forth below. Linden Lab may or may not charge fees for the right to acquire, transfer or access Virtual Land, and these fees may change at any time.

When you acquire Virtual Land, Linden Lab hereby grants you a limited license ('Virtual Land License') to access and use features of the Service associated with the virtual unit(s) of space corresponding to the identifiers of the Virtual Land within the Service as designated by Linden Lab, in accordance with these Terms of Service and any other applicable policies, including the Second Life Mainland Policies as they exist from time to time. The Virtual Land License is transferable by the holder to any other user provided that both users and the proposed transfer comply with these Terms of Service, maintain their accounts in good standing, and are not delinquent on any Account payment requirements. Except as expressly permitted by this Agreement, this Virtual Land License may not otherwise be encumbered, conveyed or made subject to any right of survivorship or other disposition and any attempted disposition in violation of these Terms of Service is null and void. Linden Lab may revoke the Virtual Land License at any time without notice, refund or compensation in the event that:

(i) Linden Lab determines that fraud, illegal conduct or any other violations of these Terms of Service or other Second Life policies is associated with the holder's Account or Virtual Land; or

(ii) the holder becomes delinquent on any of that user's Account's payment requirements, ceases to maintain an active Account or terminates this Agreement.

You may permit or deny other users to access your Virtual Land on terms determined by you. Any agreement you make with other users relating to use or access to your Virtual Land must be consistent with these Terms of Service, and no such agreement can abrogate, nullify, void or modify these Terms of Service.

You acknowledge that Virtual Land is a limited license right and is not a real property right or actual real estate, and it is not redeemable for any sum of money from Linden Lab. You acknowledge that the use of the words 'Buy,' 'Sell' and similar terms carry the same meaning of referring to the transfer of the Virtual Land License as they do with respect to the Linden Dollar License. You agree that Linden Lab has the right to manage, regulate, control, modify and/or eliminate such Virtual Land as it sees fit and that Linden Lab shall have no liability to you based on its exercise of such right. Linden Lab makes no guarantee as to the nature of the features of the Service that will be accessible through the use of Virtual Land, or the availability or supply of Virtual Land.

Return to top

7. Content licenses and intellectual property rights

7.1 You retain any and all Intellectual Property Rights in Content you submit to the Service

You retain any and all Intellectual Property Rights you already hold under applicable law in Content you upload, publish, and submit to or through the Servers, Websites, and other areas of the Service, subject to the rights, licenses, and other terms of this Agreement, including any underlying rights of other users or Linden Lab in Content that you may use or modify.

In connection with Content you upload, publish, or submit to any part of the Service, you affirm, represent, and warrant that you own or have all necessary Intellectual Property Rights, licenses, consents, and permissions to use and authorize Linden Lab and users of *Second Life* to use the Content in the manner contemplated by the Service and these Terms of Service.

Because the law may or may not recognize certain Intellectual Property Rights in any particular Content, you should consult a lawyer if you want legal advice regarding your legal rights in a specific situation. You acknowledge and agree that you are responsible for knowing, protecting, and enforcing any Intellectual Property Rights you hold, and that Linden Lab cannot do so on your behalf.

7.2 You grant certain Content licenses to Linden Lab by submitting your Content to the Service

You agree that by uploading, publishing, or submitting any Content to or through the Servers, Websites, or other areas of the Service, you hereby automatically grant Linden Lab a non-exclusive, worldwide, royalty-free, sublicenseable, and transferable license to use, reproduce, distribute, prepare derivative works of, display, and perform the Content solely for the purposes of providing and promoting the Service.

You understand that this license enables Linden Lab to display, distribute, promote, and improve the Service. You agree that the license includes the right to copy, analyze and use any of your Content as Linden Lab may deem necessary or desirable for purposes of debugging, testing, or providing support or development services in connection with the Service and future improvements to the Service. The license granted in this Section 7.2 is referred to as the 'Service Content License.'

7.3 You grant certain Content licenses to users of *Second Life* by submitting your Content to publicly accessible areas of the Service

You agree that by uploading, publishing, or submitting any Content to any publicly accessible areas of the Service, you hereby grant each user of *Second Life* a non-exclusive license to access the User Content through the Service, and to use, reproduce, distribute, prepare derivative works of, display, and perform the Content Inworld or otherwise on the Service solely as permitted by you through your interactions with the Service under these Terms of Service. This license is referred to as the 'User Content License,' and the Content being licensed is referred to as 'User Content.'

'Publicly accessible' areas of the Service are those areas that are accessible to other users of *Second Life*. If you do not wish to grant users of *Second Life* a User Content License, you agree that it is your obligation to avoid displaying or making available your Content to other users. For example, you may use Virtual Land tools to limit or restrict other users' access to your Virtual Land and thus the Content on your Virtual Land.

'Your interactions with the Service' may include use of the *Second Life* permissions system and the copy, modify, and transfer settings for indicating how other users may use, reproduce, distribute, prepare derivative works of, display, or perform your Content Inworld subject to these Terms of Service. Any agreement you make with other users relating to use or access to your Content must be consistent with these Terms of Service, and no such agreement can abrogate, nullify, void or modify these Terms of Service.

You acknowledge that when you receive a User Content License you receive only licensing and use rights: You therefore do not acquire ownership of any copies of the Content, or transfer of any copyright or other Intellectual Property Rights in the Content. You acknowledge that with respect to the use of the words 'Buy' and 'Sell' as used in this Agreement and throughout the Service in the context of User Content: (a) the term 'Sell' means 'to grant a User Content License in exchange for Linden dollars or other consideration in accordance with the Terms of Service,' (b) the term 'Buy' or 'Purchase' means 'to receive a User Content License in exchange for Linden dollars or other consideration in accordance with the Terms of Service,' and (c) the terms 'Buyer,' 'Seller,' 'Sale' and 'Purchaser' and similar terms have corresponding meanings to their root terms. This includes User Content that may be Bought or Sold on the Xstreet SL online marketplace.

7.4 You also grant Linden Lab and other users of *Second Life* a license to use in snapshots and machinima your Content that is displayed Inworld in publicly accessible areas of the Service

You agree that by uploading, publishing, or submitting any Content to or through the Servers for display Inworld in any publicly accessible area of the Service, you hereby grant each user of *Second Life* and Linden Lab a non-exclusive, worldwide, royalty-free, sublicenseable and transferable license to photograph, capture an image of, film, and record a video of the Content, and to use, reproduce, distribute, prepare derivative works of, display, and perform the resulting photograph, image, film, or video in any current or future media as provided in and subject to the restrictions and requirements of our Snapshot and Machinima Policy. The foregoing license is referred to as the 'Snapshot and Machinima Content License.'

'Publicly accessible' areas of the Service are those areas that are accessible to other users of *Second Life*. If you do not wish to grant users of *Second Life* a Snapshot and Machinima Content License, you agree that it is your obligation to avoid displaying or making available your Content to other users. For example, you may use Virtual Land tools to limit or restrict other users' access to your Virtual Land and thus the Content on your Virtual Land.

7.5 You may delete copies of your Content from the Service, and the licenses you have granted for the deleted copies will terminate with certain limitations

You may delete copies or instances of your Content that you have displayed Inworld or that are in your Account inventory through the normal functionality of the Service, including by emptying the trash folder in your Account inventory. In such event, the licenses granted by you in this Section 7 shall terminate in the manner provided below, but only for those particular copies or instances of Content that you have deleted from the Service.

You acknowledge that this termination will not apply to any other copies or instances of the same Content that you have not specifically deleted from the Service, including without limitation those that may be displayed elsewhere Inworld and those that may be in the Account inventories of other users to whom you transferred copies.

You acknowledge that the Snapshot and Machinima Content License granted to Linden Lab and other users with respect to your Content will survive any such termination.

You also acknowledge that the Service Content License granted to Linden Lab with respect to your Content will survive any such termination solely as follows to permit Linden Lab:

(i) to retain server copies of particular instances of your Content, including copies stored in connection with back-up, debugging, and testing procedures; and

(ii) to enable the exercise of the licenses granted in this Section 7 for any other copies or instances of the same Content that you have not specifically deleted from the Service, including those that may be displayed elsewhere Inworld or exist in other users' Account inventories.

7.6 Linden Lab owns Intellectual Property Rights in and to the Service, except all User Content, and in and to the Linden Marks

Linden Lab owns Intellectual Property Rights in and to the Service, except all User Content, including the Linden Software, the Websites, the Servers, and the Linden Inworld Content, and in and to our trademarks, service marks, trade names, logos, domain names, taglines, and trade dress (collectively, the 'Linden Marks'). You understand that such Intellectual Property Rights are apart from any rights you may have in Content you upload, publish or submit to the Service, as discussed above. You acknowledge and agree that Linden Lab and its licensors own all right, title, and interest in and to the Service, including all Intellectual Property Rights therein, other than with respect to User Content.

Use of the Linden Marks in whole or in part, including without limitation '*Second Life*,' 'SL,' 'Linden,' and the Eye-in-Hand logo, is subject to the guidelines and terms of any applicable license provided in our Second Life Brand Center and Trademark Guidelines. You understand and agree that without a written license agreement with Linden Lab, we do not authorize you to make any use of the Linden Marks.

Certain of the fonts in the Meta family of copyrighted typefaces are used in *Second Life* under license from FSI FontShop International. You acknowledge that you may not copy any Meta font that is included in the Viewer and that you may use any such Meta font solely to the extent necessary to use the Linden Software in *Second Life* and that you will not use such Meta fonts for any other purpose whatsoever.

Except as expressly granted in this Agreement, all rights, title, and interest in and to the Service, except all User Content, and in and to the Linden Marks are reserved by Linden Lab. Copyright, trademark and other laws of the United States and foreign countries protect the Service and the Linden Marks.

7.7 Linden Lab grants you certain licenses to access and use *Second Life* while you are in full compliance with the Terms of Service

Linden Lab hereby grants you a non-exclusive, non-transferable, non-sublicenseable, limited, revocable license to access and use the Service as set forth in these Terms of Service and expressly conditioned upon you and each of your Accounts remaining active, in good standing, and in full compliance with these Terms of Service. Additional terms may apply to certain elements of the Service; these terms are available where such separate elements are made available on the Websites. If there is any contradiction between any additional terms and these Terms of Service, then the additional terms shall take precedence only in relation to that particular element of the Service.

Use of the Linden Software is subject to these Terms of Service and the terms of any applicable End User License Agreement (EULA) provided with such software. With respect to the source code for the Viewer and any other Linden Software that has been released by Linden Lab under an open source license, such software source code must be used in accordance with the applicable open source license terms and conditions.

If no EULA is provided with any Linden Software, such software is subject to the license terms set forth in this Section. Linden Lab hereby grants you a nonexclusive, non-transferable, non-sublicensable, revocable, limited license to install and use the object code of the Linden

Software on any computer that you own or control. You may not charge any third party for using the Linden Software, and you may not modify, adapt, reverse engineer (except as otherwise permitted by applicable law notwithstanding such limitation), decompile or attempt to discover the source code of the Linden Software, or create any derivative works of the Linden Software, or otherwise use the Linden Software except as expressly provided in this Agreement.

Linden Lab provides access to Linden Inworld Content and hereby grants you a non-exclusive, non-transferable, non-sublicensable, limited, revocable license to use, reproduce, distribute, prepare derivative works of, display, and perform the Linden Inworld Content solely Inworld as permitted through the normal functionality of the Service and under these Terms of Service, except that photographs, images, films, and videos of Linden Inworld Content may be used in other areas of and outside the Service as provided in our Snapshot and Machinima Policy. To be clear, and without limiting the foregoing, you may not use, reproduce, distribute, prepare derivative works of, display or perform any Linden Inworld Content, whether modified by you or not, outside the virtual world environment of the Service except as provided in the Snapshot and Machinima Policy or as expressly agreed upon in a written agreement with Linden Lab. The foregoing license is referred to as a 'Linden Inworld Content License.'

You acknowledge that when you receive a Linden Inworld Content License you do not acquire ownership of any copies of the Content, or transfer of any copyright or other intellectual property rights in the Content.

Any access to or use of the Service through a software client other than the Linden Software that logs into the Servers (referred to as a 'Third-Party Viewer') is subject to these Terms of Service and the terms of the Policy on Third-Party Viewers. The Policy on Third-Party Viewers provides required and prohibited functionality for Third-Party Viewers as well as other terms for those who use, develop, or distribute Third-Party Viewers; however, Linden Lab offers and supports the Service only as offered by Linden Lab and is not obligated to allow access to or use of the Service by any software or means not provided by Linden Lab. You understand and agree that Linden Lab is not responsible or liable for any aspect of the Service that is accessed or experienced using software or other means not provided by Linden Lab.

Any use of the Service, including Content on the Service, other than as specifically authorized in this Agreement, without the prior written permission of Linden Lab, is strictly prohibited and will terminate all licenses granted herein.

7.8 You agree to respect the Intellectual Property Rights of other users, Linden Lab, and third parties

You agree that you will not upload, publish, or submit to any part of the Service any Content that is protected by Intellectual Property Rights or otherwise subject to proprietary rights, including trade secret or privacy rights, unless you are the owner of such rights or have permission from the rightful owner to upload, publish, or submit the Content and to grant Linden Lab and users of the Service all of the license rights granted in these Terms of Service.

You acknowledge that the Content of the Service is provided or made available to you under license from Linden Lab and independent Content providers, including other users of the Service ('Content Providers'). You acknowledge and agree that except as expressly provided in this Agreement, the Intellectual Property Rights of Linden Lab and other Content Providers in their respective Content are not licensed to you by your mere use of the Service. You must obtain from the applicable Content Providers any necessary license rights in Content that you desire to use or access.

Linden Lab and other Content Providers may use the normal functionality of the Service, including the permissions system and the copy, modify, and transfer settings, to indicate how you may use, reproduce, distribute, prepare derivative works of, display, or perform their respective Content solely Inworld. You acknowledge and agree that the permissions system and other functionality of the Service do not grant you any license, consent, or permission to copy, modify, transfer, or use in any manner any Content outside the Service.

You agree that you will not copy, transfer, or distribute outside the Service any Content that contains any Linden Inworld Content, in whole or in part or in modified or unmodified form, except as allowed by the Snapshot and Machinima Policy, or that infringes or violates any Intellectual Property Rights of Linden Lab, other Content Providers, or any third parties.

Linden Lab reserves the right, but is not obligated to use technological measures designed to prohibit the copying, transfer, or distribution of Content outside the Service when we in good faith believe that such copying, transfer, or distribution would or might violate the Intellectual Property Rights of our users, Linden Lab, or third parties.

You copy and use Content at your own risk. You are solely responsible and liable for your use, reproduction, distribution, modification, display, or performance of any Content in violation of any Intellectual Property

Rights. You agree that Linden Lab will have no liability for, and you agree to defend, indemnify, and hold Linden Lab harmless for, any claims, losses or damages arising out of or in connection with your use, reproduction, distribution, modification, display, or performance of any Content.

Return to top

8. *Conduct by users of* Second Life

8.1 You agree to abide by certain rules of conduct, including the Community Standards and other rules prohibiting illegal and other practices that Linden Lab deems harmful

You agree to read and comply with the Community Standards posted on the applicable areas of the Websites (for users 18 years of age and older; and for users of Teen *Second Life*, the Teen Community Standards).

8.2 You will not post or transmit prohibited Content, including any Content that is illegal, harassing or violates any person's rights

You agree that you will not:

(i) Post, display or transmit Content that violates any law, or the rights of any third party including without limitation Intellectual Property Rights;

(ii) Impersonate any person or entity without their consent, or otherwise misrepresent your affiliation;

(iii) Post, display or transmit any material, object or text that encourages, represents, or facilitates sexual 'age play,' i.e., using child-like avatars in a sexualized manner. This activity is grounds for immediate termination. You may review our full Age Play Policy here. You understand and agree that we may report any and all such incidents – and any and all of your corresponding personal information – to any authorities we deem appropriate, whether or not it in and of itself violates the law of your (or any) jurisdiction;

(iv) Post, display or transmit Content that is harmful, threatening or harassing, defamatory, libelous, false, inaccurate, misleading, or invades another person's privacy;

(v) Post, display or transmit Content that is obscene, hateful, or racially, ethnically or otherwise objectionable;

(vi) Operate or profit from a 'game of chance' In Second Life. For more information please see our Gambling Policy;

(vii) Operate or profit from a virtual 'bank' In Second Life. For more information please see our Banking Policy; or

(viii) Post, display or transmit any Content that is explicitly sexual, intensely violent or otherwise designated as Adult under our Maturity ratings, except as set forth in those ratings.

Any violation by you of the terms of this Section may result in immediate suspension or termination of your Accounts without any refund or other compensation.

8.3 You agree that you will not post or transmit Content or code that may be harmful, impede other users' functionality, invade other users' privacy, or surreptitiously or negatively impact any system or network

You agree to respect both the integrity of the Service and the privacy of other users. You will not:

(i) Post or transmit viruses, Trojan horses, worms, spyware, time bombs, cancelbots, or other computer programming routines that may harm the Service or interests or rights of other users, or that may harvest or collect any data or personal information about other users without their consent;

(ii) Post or transmit unsolicited or unauthorized advertising, or promotional materials, that are in the nature of 'junk mail,' 'spam,' 'chain letters,' 'pyramid schemes,' or any other form of solicitation that Linden Lab considers to be of such nature;

(iii) Use robots or other automated means to increase traffic to any Virtual Land;

(iv) Engage in malicious or disruptive conduct that impedes or interferes with other users' normal use of the Service;

(v) Attempt to gain unauthorized access to any other user's Account, password, Virtual Land or Content; or

(vi) Violate our Second Life Mainland Policies, each of which is incorporated into this Agreement.

Any violation by you of the terms of this Section may result in immediate suspension or termination of your Accounts without any refund or other compensation.

Return to top

9. *Privacy and your personal information*

We are committed to protecting your privacy and will use your information only as described in our Privacy Policy.

Our Privacy Policy sets forth the conditions under which you provide personal and other information to us. You understand and agree that through your use of the Service you consent to the collection and use of your information in accordance with our Privacy Policy. If you object to your information being used in this way, please do not use the Service.

Return to top

10. *Releases, disclaimers, liability limits and indemnification*

10.1 Linden Lab is NOT liable for its users' actions, and you release Linden Lab from any claims relating to other users

You agree not to hold Linden Lab liable for the Content, actions, or inactions of other users. As a condition of access to the Service, you release Linden Lab (and its officers, directors, shareholders, agents, subsidiaries, and employees) from claims, demands, losses, liabilities and damages (actual and consequential) of every kind and nature, known and unknown, arising out of or in any way connected with any dispute you have or claim to have with one or more users, including whether or not Linden Lab becomes involved in any resolution or attempted resolution of the dispute. If you are a California resident, you waive California Civil Code Section 1542, which says: 'A general release does not extend to claims which the creditor does not know or suspect to exist in his favor at the time of executing the release, which if known by him must have materially affected his settlement with the debtor.' If you are a resident of another jurisdiction, you waive any comparable statute or doctrine.

You agree and understand that Linden Lab does not control and is not responsible for information you provide to parties other than Linden Lab.

10.2 Linden Lab provides the Service on an 'as is' basis, without express or implied warranties, and all Content, Linden dollars and Virtual Land have no guarantee or warranty of any compensable value

LINDEN LAB PROVIDES THE SERVICE, INCLUDING WITHOUT LIMITATION THE LINDEN SOFTWARE, THE WEBSITES, THE SERVERS, THE LINDEN INWORLD CONTENT, AND YOUR ACCOUNT, STRICTLY ON AN 'AS IS' BASIS, AND HEREBY EXPRESSLY DISCLAIMS ALL WARRANTIES OR CONDITIONS OF ANY KIND, WRITTEN OR ORAL, EXPRESS, IMPLIED OR STATUTORY, INCLUDING WITHOUT LIMITATION ANY IMPLIED WARRANTY OF TITLE, NONINFRINGEMENT, MERCHANTABILITY OR FITNESS FOR A PARTICULAR PURPOSE.

NO VALUE, EITHER EXPRESS OR IMPLIED, IS GUARANTEED OR WARRANTED WITH RESPECT TO ANY CONTENT, LINDEN DOLLARS OR VIRTUAL LAND. NOTWITHSTANDING ANY INTELLECTUAL PROPERTY RIGHTS YOU MAY HAVE IN YOUR CONTENT OR ANY EXPENDITURE ON YOUR PART, LINDEN LAB AND YOU EXPRESSLY DISCLAIM ANY COMPENSABLE VALUE RELATING TO OR ATTRIBUTABLE TO ANY DATA RELATING TO YOUR ACCOUNT RESIDING ON LINDEN LAB'S SERVERS. YOU ASSUME ALL RISK OF LOSS FROM USING THE SERVICE ON THIS BASIS.

Linden Lab does not ensure continuous, error-free, secure or virus-free operation of the Service, the Linden Software, the Websites, the Servers, or your Account, and you understand that you shall not be entitled to refunds or other compensation based on Linden Lab's failure to provide any of the foregoing other than as explicitly provided in this Agreement. Some jurisdictions do not allow the disclaimer of implied warranties, and to that extent, the foregoing disclaimer may not apply to you.

10.3 Linden Lab's liability to you is expressly limited, to the extent allowable under applicable law

IN NO EVENT SHALL LINDEN LAB OR ANY OF ITS DIRECTORS, OFFICERS, EMPLOYEES, SHAREHOLDERS, SUBSIDIARIES, AGENTS OR LICENSORS BE LIABLE TO YOU OR TO ANY THIRD PARTY FOR ANY SPECIAL, INCIDENTAL, INDIRECT, CONSEQUENTIAL, RELIANCE,

PUNITIVE OR EXEMPLARY DAMAGES OR DISGORGEMENT OR COMPARABLE EQUITABLE REMEDY, INCLUDING WITHOUT LIMITATION ANY DAMAGES FOR LOST DATA OR LOST PROFITS, ARISING (WHETHER IN CONTRACT, TORT, STRICT LIABILITY OR OTHERWISE) OUT OF OR IN CONNECTION WITH THE SERVICE (INCLUDING ITS MODIFICATION OR TERMINATION), THE LINDEN SOFTWARE, THE WEBSITES, THE SERVERS, YOUR ACCOUNT (INCLUDING ITS TERMINATION OR SUSPENSION) OR THIS AGREEMENT, WHETHER OR NOT LINDEN LAB MAY HAVE BEEN ADVISED THAT ANY SUCH DAMAGES MIGHT OR COULD OCCUR AND NOTWITHSTANDING THE FAILURE OF ESSENTIAL PURPOSE OF ANY REMEDY.

IN NO EVENT WILL LINDEN LAB'S CUMULATIVE LIABILITY TO YOU EXCEED THE GREATER OF

(i) ONE HUNDRED DOLLARS (U.S. $100.00); OR

(ii) THE RELEVANT AMOUNT SET FORTH IN SECTION 11 HEREIN, IF APPLICABLE.

Some jurisdictions do not allow the foregoing limitations of liability, so to the extent that any such limitation is found to be impermissible, such limitation may not apply to you.

10.4 You agree to indemnify Linden Lab from claims relating to your use of the Service

At Linden Lab's request, you agree to defend, indemnify and hold harmless Linden Lab, its officers, directors, shareholders, employees, subsidiaries, and agents from all damages, liabilities, claims and expenses, including without limitation attorneys' fees and costs, arising from:

(i) any breach or alleged breach by you of this Agreement, including without limitation your representations and warranties relating to your Content; or

(ii) your acts, omissions or use of the Service, including without limitation your negligent, willful or illegal conduct. We reserve the right to assume the exclusive defense and control of any matter otherwise subject to indemnification by you, and in such case, you agree to cooperate with our defense of such claim.

10.5 You are not our employee, and you have no rights to compensation

You acknowledge that your participation in the Service, including your creation or uploading of Content in the Service, does not make you a Linden Lab employee and that you do not expect to be, and will not be, compensated by Linden Lab for such activities, and you will make no claim inconsistent with these acknowledgements. In addition, no agency, partnership, joint venture, franchise relationship is intended or created by this Agreement.

Return to top

11. Suspension and termination of your account

11.1 You may terminate your Accounts at any time

You may terminate this Agreement by closing your Accounts at any time for any reason. In such event, Linden Lab shall have no further obligation or liability to you under this Agreement or otherwise, and you shall be entitled to no compensation or other payment, remedy, recourse or refund.

11.2 You may terminate your Accounts within thirty days of any Material Change to this Agreement

These Terms of Service shall be effective upon the conclusion of the thirty (30) day period described in Section 1 above. If you do not wish to agree and abide by these Terms of Service, you have thirty (30) days to terminate your Accounts as described in Section 11.1 and conclude any outstanding *Second Life*, LindeX or related transactions. In such event, Linden Lab shall have no further obligation or liability to you under this Agreement or otherwise, and you shall not be entitled to any compensation or other payment, remedy, recourse or refund.

11.3 We may suspend or terminate your Accounts for violation of this Agreement. Your rights to any compensation or recourse are limited to those provided herein

Linden Lab may suspend or terminate your Account if you violate this Agreement, along with any or all other Accounts held by you or otherwise related to you as determined by Linden Lab, and your violation of this Agreement shall be deemed to apply to all such Accounts. Upon termination of your Accounts, this Agreement between us will be automatically terminated and you may not re-subscribe to *Second Life*, or return to *Second Life* through other or future Accounts you or others may set up. In the event of termination by Linden Lab of your Accounts under this Section 11.3, you will be entitled to receive the stated current value of any credit balance held in your Account(s), i.e., amounts you have cashed out on the LindeX, as your exclusive remedy and our sole liability. This does not include any Linden dollar balance held in your Account(s). In order to receive any sums pursuant to this Section 11.3, you must establish and inform us of a verified PayPal account into which we may transfer those sums. We will deduct from any or all of the above sums any outstanding fees or charges due to Linden Lab.

We reserve the right to impose reasonable procedures and restrictions with respect to the above, including without limitation the right to verify your identity and Accounts, to limit transfers to verified PayPal accounts, to impose other anti-fraud measures, and to refuse to process funds we believe are the product of fraud or theft.

11.4 We may suspend or terminate your Account(s) to protect the best interests of *Second Life* and the *Second Life* community or if we believe you pose an unacceptable risk to the Second Life community

We may suspend or terminate your Account if we determine in our discretion that such action is necessary or advisable to comply with legal requirements or protect the rights or interests of Linden Lab, the *Second Life* community or any third party.

We may suspend or terminate your Account(s) if we learn, or in good faith believe, that you are a Registered Sex Offender, that accessing *Second Life* may violate a condition of parole or probation, or that you for any other reason may pose what we deem to be an unacceptable risk to the *Second Life* community.

11.5 We may suspend or terminate your Accounts upon a general suspension or discontinuation of the Service

If Linden Lab elects to generally suspend or discontinue the Service, in whole or in part, for any reason, Linden Lab may suspend or terminate your Accounts. In such event, except as described in Section 11.3, you will not be entitled to compensation for such suspension or termination, and you acknowledge Linden Lab will have no liability to you in connection with such suspension or termination. You acknowledge and agree that a general suspension or discontinuation of the Service, in whole or in part, for any reason, will not constitute a Material Change requiring advance notice.

11.6 You will lose access to your Account and all licenses, Content, and data upon termination, and you understand this is a risk of participating in the Service

Upon termination of your Account, you will no longer be able to access your Account or access (or transfer or direct the transfer to any other Account) any Content or data you have stored on the Servers. All licenses granted by Linden Lab to use the Service, including without limitation any Linden Dollar Licenses and any Virtual Land Licenses will automatically terminate. You acknowledge that you have elected to procure Linden Dollar Licenses or Virtual Land Licenses or any premium account or paid features of the Services notwithstanding the possibility of termination of such license rights under the circumstances set forth in this Agreement.

You should ensure that you have only stored Content on the Servers to which you are willing to permanently lose access. You acknowledge and assume the risk of the possibility of suspension or termination of your Account as provided herein, and you represent that you will make your decisions to participate in the Service, contribute Content, spend your money and dispose of transferable licenses at all times knowingly based upon these risks.

Upon termination, you will remain liable for any unpaid amounts owed by you to Linden Lab and Linden Lab has the right to set off any amounts owed by you or for which you are otherwise liable against any compensation that you may be entitled to under this Section 11.

11.7 Some terms of this Agreement will survive and continue after termination

The following terms will survive any termination of this Agreement: Sections 7, 10, 11, 12 and 13.

Return to top

12. Dispute resolution and arbitration

12.1 If a dispute arises between you and Linden Lab regarding a claim for less than $10,000, either party may resolve it through Arbitration instead of Litigation

Our goal is to provide you with a neutral and cost-effective means of resolving the dispute quickly.

Thus, for any claim related to this Agreement or our Service, excluding claims for injunctive or other equitable relief, where the total amount sought is less than ten thousand U.S. Dollars ($10,000.00 USD), either we or you may elect at any point in or during a dispute or proceeding to resolve the claim through binding non-appearance-based arbitration. A party electing arbitration shall initiate it through an established alternative dispute resolution ('ADR') provider mutually agreed upon by the parties. The ADR provider and the parties must comply with the following rules:

(a) the arbitration shall be conducted, at the option of the party seeking relief, by telephone, online, or based solely on written submissions;

(b) the arbitration shall not involve any personal appearance by the parties or witnesses unless otherwise mutually agreed by the parties; and

(c) any judgment on the award rendered by the arbitrator may be entered in any court of competent jurisdiction.

12.2 The applicable law and venue for any non-arbitrated dispute is California

You agree that this Agreement and the relationship between you and Linden Lab shall be governed by the laws of the State of California without regard to conflict of law principles or the United Nations Convention on the International Sale of Goods. Further, you and Linden Lab agree to submit to the exclusive jurisdiction and venue of the courts located in the City and County of San Francisco, California, except as provided in Section 12.1 regarding optional arbitration. Notwithstanding this, either party shall still be allowed to apply for injunctive or other equitable relief to protect or enforce that party's Intellectual Property Rights in any court of competent jurisdiction where the other party resides or has its principal place of business.

12.3 Improperly Filed Claims are Subject to Attorneys' Fees and Costs

All claims you bring against Linden Lab must be resolved in accordance with this Dispute Resolution and Arbitration Section. All claims filed or brought contrary to this Dispute Resolution Section shall be considered improperly filed and a breach of these Terms of Service. Should either party file a claim contrary to this Dispute Resolution Section, the other party may recover attorneys' fees and costs up to one thousand U.S. Dollars ($1,000.00 USD), provided that such party seeking such fees has notified the other in writing of the improperly filed Claim, and the other has failed to promptly withdraw the Claim.

Return to top

13. General provisions

13.1 *Second Life* is a United States-based service

Linden Lab makes no representation that any aspect of the Service is appropriate or available for use outside of the United States. Those who access the Service from other locations are responsible for compliance with applicable local laws. The Linden Software is subject to applicable export laws and restrictions.

13.2 You may not assign your Account; we may assign this Agreement

You may not assign this Agreement or your Account without the prior written consent of Linden Lab. You may not transfer or sublicense any licenses granted by Linden Lab in this Agreement without the prior written consent of Linden Lab, except solely to the extent this Agreement permits transfer of the Linden Dollar Licenses and Virtual Land Licenses. Linden Lab may assign this Agreement, in whole or in part, and all related rights, licenses, benefits and obligations, without restriction, including the right to sublicense any rights and licenses under this Agreement.

13.3 This Agreement and the referenced Policies are the entire understanding between us

This Agreement, including the additional terms and policies referenced in Section 14, sets forth the entire understanding and agreement between you and Linden Lab with respect to the subject matter hereof and supersedes any prior or contemporaneous agreements or understandings. This Agreement may not be modified except as provided in Section 1 or by mutual written agreement between you and Linden Lab that is signed by hand (not electronically) by duly authorized representatives of both parties and expressly references amendment of this Agreement.

You acknowledge that no other written, oral or electronic communications will serve to modify or supplement this Agreement, and you agree not to make any claims inconsistent with this understanding or in reliance on communications not part of this Agreement. The section headings used herein, including descriptive summary sentences at the start of each section, are for convenience only and shall not affect the interpretation of this Agreement. As used in this Agreement, references to a determination made in Linden Lab's discretion means that the determination will be made by Linden Lab in accordance with its good faith business judgment. If any provision of this Agreement shall be held by a court of competent jurisdiction to be unlawful, void, or unenforceable, then in such jurisdiction that provision shall be deemed severable from these terms and shall not affect the validity and enforceability of the remaining provisions.

13.4 We agree to provide each other with notices in a specified manner

Linden Lab may give notice to and obtain consent from you by one or more of the following means: through the website at http://secondlife.com, through the Second Life Viewer at or after log-in to your Account, by electronic mail to your e-mail address in our records, or by written mail communication to the address on record for your Account. All notices given by you or required under this Agreement shall be faxed to Linden Lab Legal Department at: (415) 243-9045 begin_of_the_skype_highlighting (415) 243-9045 end_of_the_skype_highlighting; or mailed to us at: Linden Lab Legal Department, 945 Battery Street, San Francisco, CA 94111.

Return to top

14. Additional terms and policies

The following additional terms and policies are incorporated by reference in and made part of this Agreement, and provide additional terms, conditions and guidelines regarding the Service.

- Linden Lab Privacy Policy
- Intellectual Property Policy
- Second Life Brand Center
- Second Life Trademark Guidelines
- Snapshot and Machinima Policy
- Second Life Fee Schedule
- Second Life Billing Policy
- Xstreet SL Billing Policy
- Community Standards
- Second Life Mainland Policies
- Teen Community Standards
- Gambling Policy
- Banking Policy
- Age Play Policy
- Maturity Ratings
- Xstreet SL Marketplace Terms
- Policy on Third-Party Viewers

Any other communications or Content made available by Linden Lab on the Service is not part of this Agreement and should not be relied upon as such, or consulted for contractual purposes, but rather is provided to assist and enhance the user experience in *Second Life*.

Runescape's Terms and Conditions

Effective Date: 19th January, 2010

Terms and Conditions

Introduction

This website is owned and operated by *Jagex* Limited ('*Jagex*'), a company registered in England and Wales (registered number 3982706). Our registered office is at St John's Innovation Centre, Cowley Road, Cambridge, CB4 0WS, United Kingdom. Our VAT number is 791 951 784.

Definitions

'*Jagex* Product(s)' is used as shorthand for our online games including all *Jagex* websites used to play those games.

References to 'Stopping' an account include all or any of: locking, temporarily or permanently banning, or temporarily or permanently muting the account. If your account is muted, you can continue to play but will not be able to use free text chat. If your account is banned, you will not be able to access your account at all. NB Membership credit continues to expire if accounts are muted or banned.

Applicability

Please read these terms and conditions carefully. Your accepting them in full is a condition of your use of a *Jagex* product (whether or not you subscribe). If you don't agree with any part, please don't accept them or use the *Jagex* product.

If you have any questions about these terms and conditions, please contact us via email at and do not use the site until you are satisfied with and can accept these terms and conditions in full.

Changes

We may change these terms and conditions to reflect: changes in applicable laws; regulatory or security requirements; relevant guidance or codes of practice; technical alterations to *Jagex* Products; and to improve clarity and consistency. Please check the terms and conditions whenever you use a *Jagex* Product. If you are not a subscriber, we will treat your continued use of a *Jagex* Product as acceptance of these changes from their effective date as shown above. If you are a subscriber, we will treat you as bound by the changes on the first renewal date for your subscription after the effective date and so you should cancel your subscription (as explained below) before this renewal date if you don't like the proposed changes.

A special note about preteens and users under 18

If you are under 13 you will be able to create an account but unable to disclose personal data through the game or website. If we find out that any personal data we have collected is from someone under 13, we will automatically delete it. We recommend that parents/guardians set up an account and play together with their children. Many parents have reported that playing *Jagex* Products as a family is fun and rewarding.

If you are under 13 and subscribe to the members' version of our game you are representing (i.e. making a promise) that you have consent from your parents/guardian to use *Jagex* Products in accordance with our terms and conditions and privacy policy. We may Stop any account if we are not satisfied that such consent has been given.

If you are under 18, by using our website you are representing (i.e. making a promise) that you have consent from your parents/guardian to use *Jagex* Products in accordance with our terms and conditions and privacy policy. We may Stop any account if we are not satisfied that such consent has been given.

If we are told by a parent/guardian that their child has lied about their age when registering for *Jagex* Products, we will Stop the account provided we have information which satisfies us that the reporting person is indeed the parent or guardian.

Parents can find more information about the game and how to contact us in the Parents' Guide.

Safety/abuse

Before using any *Jagex* Product you should read the guides found in our Safety & Security Guidelines. It is particularly important to read the Play Safely Guide and the Health & Safety Guide. Parents should review our safety materials in the Player Safety section of the Parents' Guide.

Whilst we reserve the right to monitor and take action if any *Jagex* Product is used inappropriately (including the posting of objectionable material on the chat facility or otherwise), we cannot promise that any *Jagex* Product won't contain such content or that we will remove/modify any particular content. Nor can we guarantee that users will comply with our terms and conditions or otherwise behave appropriately.

If you are the victim of offensive or inappropriate behavior or receive any other unwanted communications, you should use the built-in facilities to block the messages. (See this article for guidance on blocking messages.) You should report all inappropriate behaviour to us via the in game 'Report abuse' button as well as seeking appropriate external help, for example from parents or law enforcement authorities. If you continue to suffer problems, or are not satisfied, then you must stop using the relevant *Jagex* Product(s).

Your account

To use many features of *Jagex* Products, we require you to create an account. We grant valid account holders a non-exclusive, non-transferable license for the period of membership to use *Jagex* Products and to download and use our client software and connect to our servers solely to use *Jagex* Products in accordance with these terms and conditions.

You must not choose a username that infringes the rights of any third party, impersonates *Jagex* staff or other users, which is deliberately confusing or which is offensive, racist, obscene, hurtful, unlawful or otherwise inappropriate or which breaches the username requirements specified on our site or our Rules of Conduct. We reserve the right to make such assessment in our sole discretion, change any username for any reason or take such other action as we believe appropriate.

You agree to keep your password safe at all times and not to disclose it to any other person. You are responsible for the activities of all persons who use your password to gain access to your account. To help ensure the safety of your password, you must keep your computer free of viruses and other malicious code including Trojans. You must use your password in accordance with the password requirements specified on our site and our Rules of Conduct. Real *Jagex* staff will never ask you for your password. If you believe that someone has stolen your password or otherwise gained access to your account – submit an Account Recovery request via the Account Recovery link on the website of any *Jagex* Product. To see our guidance about password security and safety practices, please click here.

Rules

You must comply with the current version of any rules, guidelines, codes of conduct or instructions specified in any *Jagex* Product including our game rules, the current version of which is linked to here.

Our rights

If, acting reasonably, we consider that our Terms and Conditions have or may have been breached, or that there has been fraudulent, unlawful or abusive activity, or that it is necessary in order to prevent or stop any harm or damage to us, to any *Jagex* Product, to other players or the general public, we may Stop (as defined above) any or all accounts of *Jagex* Products which we think are connected with the offender subject to such right of appeal as is specified on our website and/or restrict access to or delete JCredits or anything acquired by means of JCredits. Such actions may result in loss of membership credit and/or loss of real money paid as part of any item/account trading or other prohibited transaction.

To prevent or remedy breach of our Terms and Conditions or any harm or damage to us, to any *Jagex* Product or to other players or the general public, we may automatically or manually monitor, censor (including rejection or removal of any content) and/or record public or private chat or other activities in any *Jagex* Product.

Intellectual property rights

Jagex®, *Runescape*® and *FunOrb*® are registered trade marks of *Jagex* Limited in the United Kingdom, the United States and other countries.

You must not reverse-engineer, decompile or modify any *Jagex* Product client software in any way (except to the extent allowed by applicable law). You must not use a modified/customised version of the client software or attempt to sub-license it. You must not create or provide any other means by which any *Jagex* Product may be played by others (including, without limitation, replacement or modified client/server software, server emulators).

Materials (including without limit all information, software, data, text, photographs, graphics, sound and video) placed on any *Jagex* Product by us or on our behalf are protected by copyright and other intellectual property rights of ourselves or our business partners/suppliers/advertisers. You may not use these materials or any *Jagex* Product except in accordance with these terms and conditions and for personal (i.e. non-commercial) use only.

You agree that all intellectual property or other rights in any game character, account and items are and will remain our property.

By posting chat or other materials on any *Jagex* Product, you grant us a non-exclusive, perpetual, worldwide, royalty free, worldwide license to use and/or modify such materials on any *Jagex* Product as we see fit.

You agree that by submitting any material of any kind to us for any purpose connected with any *Jagex* Product (non-exhaustive examples are suggestions and ideas for any game or contributions to any Gallery page), you are giving us a non-exclusive, perpetual, worldwide, royalty-free license to use and/or modify the submitted materials as we see fit. You agree to waive any moral rights to the extent permitted by law and that you will not withdraw the submission or attempt to make a charge for its use. Furthermore you guarantee that you are the exclusive copyright holder in relation to the submission and that the submission in no way breaches the rights of any other person or entity.

Subscription

You need a subscription to use certain features of *Jagex* Products. If you apply for a subscription, you must ensure all the information that you submit is true and accurate (including without limit your credit card number and expiration date, and other payment details) and that you have appropriate parental or guardian consent as applicable. You agree to pay all subscription fees specified when you apply including all applicable taxes. Unless otherwise stated, all prices shown for EU countries include VAT.

By submitting your order you are making an offer to subscribe to the relevant part of the *Jagex* Product(s). Your offer is accepted and a binding contract occurs when we send a message to your account mail inbox confirming that your payment has been received or if you log into a subscribers-only part of a *Jagex* Product (whichever comes first).

All subscription payments will continue to be taken in advance at the relevant intervals (e.g. monthly in the case of monthly subscriptions) until you cancel your subscription (see below).

Payments by credit cards are also subject to our credit card agreement that forms part of these terms and conditions.

We reserve the right to alter the amount or terms of our subscription fees at any time. This will only apply to those who, following the change, take out new subscriptions or re-subscribe (their previous subscriptions having expired) and specifically agree to the new fees/terms.

We reserve the right to charge you for any unauthorized use of your subscription by third parties.

Cancellation by you

You may cancel your subscription at any time by clicking here or selecting the 'Cancel Subscription' link from the account management section on the website of any *Jagex* Product.

Upon cancellation you will not be charged any further subscription fees. No payments already made will be refunded (wholly or partly) but you can of course use up any unused membership credit in the account.

For important information about the legal cancellation rights of EU consumers, please click here.

JCredits

In certain of our games, we offer JCredits for sale or, in our discretion, as free promotions. JCredits can be redeemed (ie used) to acquire certain digital goods/services, which we describe below as 'Items'. If you obtain JCredits, you must check that they have been correctly credited to your account and tell us immediately if not.

NB: JCredits are subject to very important restrictions:

JCredits expire and will be deleted if they have not been redeemed within a certain period after acquisition so you should redeem them as soon as possible. The expiry period is whatever we specify when you acquire the JCredits or, if we haven't specified a time limit, three months from acquisition.

Unless we say otherwise on our website, JCredits can only be redeemed within the world of the game where you acquired them. We may at any time change or remove any or any type of Item for which JCredits can be redeemed as well as the amount of JCredits needed to acquire a particular Item. You may only redeem JCredits for Items on offer at the time of redemption.

JCredits do not have any inherent value and they are not your own private property. You can only use them to acquire those Items that we decide in our discretion to offer in return for JCredits. We do not provide any cash or refunds for JCredits (except as required by law). JCredits are for your personal use only. You must not sell or transfer them or make them available to anyone else or attempt to do so or encourage anyone else to do any of these things.

We may impose additional restrictions concerning the acquisition or redemption of JCredits. For example we may cap the amount of JCredits that can be acquired or held or redeemed in any particular period or we may impose restrictions based on your country of residence.

We may restrict access to or delete JCredits or Items:

(1) as outlined under 'Our Rights' above;

(2) if the JCredits were awarded in error; or

(3) if a payment for JCredits is charged back or otherwise cancelled or reversed.

We may at any time decide to end the entire JCredit program for all or any of our games. Before we delete the unused JCredits, we will endeavour to give you at least four weeks to redeem them.

Privacy policy

For a description of how we use your personal data, please see our Privacy policy.

Functioning of Jagex *Products*

We will do our best to maintain operation of *Jagex* Products and rectify faults as quickly as possible. We may have to suspend operation of a *Jagex* Product without notice for repair, maintenance, improvement or other technical reason. If so, we will do our best to ensure that the suspension is as short as possible. We cannot accept responsibility for such suspensions or for any interruption or error caused by circumstances outside our reasonable control.

We cannot guarantee that *Jagex* Products will work with any particular computer equipment or in conjunction with any particular software or connectivity services. We do not accept responsibility for such equipment, software or services.

Third parties

Jagex Products may include links to internet sites or other technologies supplied by third parties including sites/technologies which enable you to pay by means of payment methods provided by third parties. We make no promises about those sites or their content, products or services as these are outside our reasonable control.

Our and your legal responsibility

WE DO NOT ACCEPT LEGAL RESPONSIBILITY FOR ANY LOSS OR DAMAGE CAUSED BY US OR OUR EMPLOYEES OR AGENTS IN CIRCUMSTANCES WHERE:

(A) THERE IS NO BREACH OF A LEGAL DUTY OF CARE OWED TO YOU BY US OR BY ANY OF OUR EMPLOYEES OR AGENTS;

(B) SUCH LOSS OR DAMAGE IS NOT A REASONABLY FORESEEABLE RESULT OF ANY SUCH BREACH; OR

(C) SUCH LOSS OR DAMAGE RELATES TO A BUSINESS.

YOU WILL BE LIABLE FOR ANY LOSS OR DAMAGE WE SUFFER ARISING FROM YOUR BREACH OF THIS AGREEMENT OR MISUSE OF A *JAGEX* PRODUCT.

Transfer

We may transfer all or part of our rights or duties under this agreement provided we take reasonable steps to ensure that your rights under this agreement are not prejudiced. As this agreement is personal to you, you may not transfer any of your rights or duties under it without our prior written consent.

General

Nothing in these terms and conditions affects your statutory rights as a consumer. Headings above are for guidance only and not binding. If we fail to enforce any provision of these terms and conditions, that failure will not preclude us from enforcing either that provision (or any similar provision) on a later occasion. If any provision of these terms and conditions is found by a court to be invalid, we agree that the court should endeavour to give effect to the parties' intentions as reflected in the provision and that other provisions remain in full force and effect. Except for clauses excluding or restricting our liability a person who is not a party to this agreement shall have no rights under the Contracts (Rights of Third Parties) Act 1999 to enforce any term of this agreement. These terms and conditions are governed by English law and any dispute connected with them or *Jagex* Products will be decided only by the courts of the United Kingdom.

Complaints

If you are dissatisfied with this website or any aspect of it, please contact us via the forms on our website or write to our registered office above.

EVE Online's Terms of Service

Website terms of use agreement

Disclaimer

This website is currently owned and operated by CCP, hf.

CCP, hf disclaims any and all responsibility or liability for the accuracy, content, completeness, legality, reliability, or operability or availability of information or material contained on the Web site. CCP, hf. disclaims any responsibility for the deletion, failure to store, misdelivery, or untimely delivery of any information or material in respect to the web site. CCP, hf. disclaims any responsibility for any harm resulting from downloading or accessing any information or material on or thorough the web site.

CCP, hf. does not warrant or represent the information on this page or to which you may link from this page is in compliance with governmental laws or regulations.

THIS AGREEMENT WAS LAST UPDATED ON, 8th of March 2007.

Age restrictions

YOU MUST BE 13 YEARS OF AGE OR OLDER TO USE THIS WEB SITE. PLEASE READ OUR AGE REQUIREMENTS IN SECTION 3.3 OF THIS AGREEMENT UNDER WHICH PARENTAL CONSENT MAY BE REQUIRED UNDER CERTAIN CONDITIONS.

PLEASE READ THE ENTIRE AGREEMENT SET OUT IN THE PAGES BELOW BEFORE PROCEEDING.

This Agreement governs your use of this web site and all of its affiliated web sites and the services they provide (collectively, the 'Web Site'). Please read it carefully before using the Web Site. By using the Web Site, you are consenting to the terms and conditions of the Agreement. If you do not consent to the terms and conditions of the Agreement, then do not use the Web Site. CCP, hf. may modify the terms and conditions of the Agreement at anytime. In such event, CCP, hf. will post the modified terms on the Web Site. The Web Site is controlled and operated by CCP, hf. from its offices in Reykjavik, Iceland and is intended for Icelander users only. CCP, hf. makes no representation that the materials on the site are appropriate or available for use in other locations. If you access the Web Site from any non-Icelandic territory, you do so at your own risk and are responsible for compliance with any local laws.

Privacy

We may use your email address to verify your identity, protect against fraud, and contact you. In addition, we may use it to send you updates about your user account, new products and services, and company updates. Otherwise, we will not request any personal information from you. Moreover, we ask that you refrain from submitting any personal information to the Web Site. Any information which is sent to the Web Site, however, is deemed a grant to CCP of a perpetual, royalty-free, irrevocable, non-exclusive worldwide right and license to use, disclose, display, exhibit, perform, reproduce, modify, adapt, publish, translate, and distribute such Content or incorporate such Content into any form, medium, or technology now known or hereafter developed. Further, CCP shall be free to use any ideas, concepts, know-how, or techniques contained in such information for any purposes whatsoever including but not limited to research, development, manufacturing, and marketing of products and other items incorporating such ideas. If you are not the owner of the Content submitted, you warrant that you have received all necessary consents from the owner of such rights. You will hold CCP harmless if any such Content submitted is in violation of any such rights.

Personal information submitted by users to the CCP website may be employed for the purposes of maintaining the integrity of the website and its contents, contacting our users when necessary, and improving the quality of service provided by CCP. Such information includes personal information about the user and details of his character, for example. CCP servers also collect information that is specific to how you use the Internet. CCP servers note details such as the server you are logged onto, the geographic location of the ISP and type of browser you use, and your IP address. This information is obtained solely for the purpose of maintaining the site's integrity and improving our service. CCP may use cookies to improve and better understand your Web browsing experience. When you first log in to certain CCP services, you may be assigned a unique random ID to your computer browser – commonly known as a 'cookie.' We do this to understand the way a user uses our site and to improve the quality of your experience with the Web Site.

Advertisers, or other CCP partners, may employ a third-party measurement service for tracking the performance of an ad program. In these instances, we have no control over the information collected by the third party, and may not be held responsible for the actions of the third party measurement service where collected information is concerned. CCP may use third-party advertising companies to serve ads when you visit our Web site. These companies may use information (not including your name, address, email address or telephone number) about your visits to this and other Web sites in order to provide advertisements on this site and other sites about goods and services that may be of interest to you. In the course of serving advertisements to this site, our third-party advertisers may place or recognize a unique 'cookie' on your browser.

We reserve the right to disclose your personally identifiable information as required by law and when we believe that disclosure is necessary to protect our rights and/or comply with a judicial proceeding, court order, or legal process served on our Web site; or to protect our company and our Members. While we make every effort to ensure the integrity and security of our network and systems, we cannot guarantee that our security measures will prevent third-party 'hackers' from illegally obtaining this information.

1. Definitions. In this Agreement, 'you' and 'your' refer to the user of the Web Site. The words 'we,' 'our' and 'us' refer to CCP, hf. 'Agreement' refers to the terms and conditions stated below, or as amended by us from time to time.
2. General. The Web Site includes a wealth of game related information, including comments, opinions, articles, advertisements, graphics, photographs, videos, forms and forums (collectively 'Content'). We provide such Content as a service to our users; however, it is not intended to serve as a substitute for any professional advice, such as legal advice. We urge you to seek advice from a competent professional before taking any action based on the Content contained on the Web Site. CCP, hf. strives to provide you quality Content; however, we make no representation as to the accuracy, completeness, timeliness or suitability of such information. It is your responsibility to evaluate the information contained on this site. CCP, hf. will not be liable for any damages resulting from your use of the information on our Web Site.
3. Restrictions.
   3.1 The Content available through the Web Site is property of CCP, hf., or of it's licensors or licensees (collectively 'CCP'). This Content is protected by trademark, copyright, and other intellectual property laws. Information received through the Web Site may be reformatted, displayed, and printed for your personal, noncommercial use on the condition that you do not change, delete, hide, remove, or in any way make ineffective the trademark, copyright, or proprietary notices therein. You agree not to reproduce, duplicate, copy, sell, rent, resell or exploit for any commercial purposes any portion of the Web Site, or access to the Web site. You agree not to create or establish, or direct any

other person to create or establish: (i) a hyperlink, including but not limited to any deep link, to any page or location on the Web Site; or (ii) a frame containing any portion of the Web Site, on any other web site or text document with hyperlink capabilities. You are, however, free to establish a hypertext link to the main or top level web page of the Web Site from your home page, provided that the link properly attributes the Web Site to CCP and does not imply any sponsorship of your site by CCP or vice versa. You may not, however, create a link that incorporates or relies upon, in whole or in part, any content from any page on the Web Site, or that incorporates any copyrights, trademarks, or other intellectual property of CCP unless you obtain the prior written consent of CCP. Requests for permission to establish links to this site may be sent via email to Webmaster@ccpgames.com or to CCP at the address listed below.

3.2 If you download software, files and images contained in or generated by software, or data accompanying software (collectively referred to as the 'Software') from the Web Site then you are deemed to have downloaded such Software solely for your personal, noncommercial home use. CCP transfers neither the title nor the intellectual property rights to the Software upon the download of the Software. Rather, CCP retains full and complete title to the Software as well as all intellectual property rights. You may neither sell, distribute, redistribute, license, nor reproduce the Software, nor may you decompile, reverse engineer, or otherwise convert the software to human-perceivable form.

3.3 Important Age Requirements. By continuing to use the Web Site, you hereby represent to CCP that you are 13 years of age or older. The age requirements differ from country to country. If you are under 20 years of age, you may need to obtain the permission of your parent(s) or legal guardian to use the Web Site. We strongly suggest that you check your local, state, province, country or regional legal restrictions that may be applicable to your use of the Web Site. See our Parental Consent Page to find out how your parent can provide consent. For example, if you are under 20 years of age and live in Japan, you may need to obtain the permission of your parent(s) or legal guardian to use the Web Site. See our Parental Consent Page to find out how. In other countries like Australia, Austria, Belgium, Canada, Denmark, France, Germany, Netherlands,

New Zealand, Norway, Portugal, Republic of Ireland, Spain, Switzerland and the United Kingdom, if you are under 18 years of age and live in one of these countries, you may need to obtain the permission of your parent(s) or legal guardian to use the Web Site. See our Parental Consent Page to find out how.

4. Modifications to Web Site. CCP reserves the right to modify or discontinue, temporarily or permanently, the Web Site (or any part thereof) from time to time, for any or no reason and without notice. You agree that CCP shall not be liable to you or to any third party for any modification, suspension or discontinuance of the Web Site. The information and materials contained on the Web Site are subject to change.
5. Links to Third Parties. The Web Site contains links to web sites created and maintained by third parties. CCP does not endorse or recommend the content, products or services provided by any such third party web sites. You understand that CCP has no control over such third-party sites, and therefore is not responsible for the content of any such third-party sites or the content of any site linked to such third party sites. CCP shall not be liable for any damage or loss caused by or in connection with the use of or reliance on any such content, products or services available on or through such third party web sites.
6. Chat, Bulletin Boards, and other Submissions.

   6.1 The Message Board service enables you to participate in chat forums on various game-related topics. You may also post a message on the Web Site's bulletin board. You acknowledge and agree that if you submit any Content to forums, you will be solely responsible for such Content. CCP will not be liable in any way for any such Content submitted. You further agree that you will not:

   I Submit any Content, which is harassing, abusive, threatening, harmful, libelous or defamatory, encourages conduct that could constitute a criminal offense or give rise to civil liabilities, or is unlawful in any other way.

   II Submit any Content protected by intellectual property laws or by rights of privacy, unless you own the rights thereto or have received all necessary consents. You shall be solely liable for any damage resulting from any infringement of copyright, trademark or other proprietary rights;

III Submit any Content that contains a virus or other harmful components;

IV Engage in activity that interferes with or disrupts the use of the Web Site by other users;

V Submit any Content that encourages any illegal activities, or provides guidance or instructional activities about such illegal activities;

VI Make any false representation, including impersonation of any person or entity or misrepresentation of your affiliation with any person or entity;

VII Make use of Message Board for commercial purposes, such as advertising any products or services, reselling or publishing the information posted or transmitted.

6.2 CCP does not prescreen, monitor or edit the Content posted or submitted to Forums. However, CCP reserves the right to edit, limit or remove any such Content in its sole discretion. Notwithstanding, you shall remain solely responsible for any Content you submit or post.

6.3 CCP may establish procedures and practices relating to the use of and participation in Forums. Such procedures and practices may include limitations on the number of entries and the size of files that may be submitted, limitations on the number of participants in any chat room at any given time and the number of days messages on the bulletin board will be saved before deletion. CCP will not be responsible for any Content deleted by CCP or otherwise, or for your inability to submit any Content.

6.4 By submitting Content, via chat or any other means, to the Web Site, you grant CCP a perpetual, royalty-free, irrevocable, non-exclusive worldwide right and license to use, disclose, display, exhibit, perform, reproduce, modify, adapt, publish, translate, and distribute such Content or incorporate such Content into any form, medium, or technology now known or hereafter developed. Further, CCP shall be free to use any ideas, concepts, know-how, or techniques contained in such information for any purposes whatsoever including but not limited to research, development, manufacturing, and marketing of products and other items incorporating such ideas. If you are not the owner of the Content submitted, you warrant that you have received all necessary consents from the owner of such rights. You will hold

CCP harmless if any such Content submitted is in violation of any such rights.

6.5 When participating in any bulletin board or chat room, you may be exposed to Content that is inaccurate, incomplete or unsuitable. You should use extra caution with respect to any Content posted or transmitted on a CCP bulletin board or chat room. CCP urges you not to take any action based on any such Content. CCP will not be responsible for the Content or accuracy of any information, and shall not be responsible for any acts taken or decisions made based on such information.

6.6 In consideration of CCP's continuing efforts to enhance and improve the Web Site and its associated products and services and to respond to feedback from users, you agree to transfer such ideas, concepts, know-how, or techniques to CCP without any compensation in return. You also agree to execute any and all documents that CCP may reasonably request in connection with confirming CCP's ownership of and unlimited right to use such ideas, concepts, know-how, and techniques.

6.7 When submitting any comments in any form to the Web Site, whether it be via chat services, bulletin board services, customer feedback email, or the like you, are solely responsible for the content of any comments you make. You agree that no comments submitted by you to the Web Site will:

I violate any right of any third party, including but not limited to copyright, trademark, privacy, or other personal or proprietary rights;

II be libelous or contain libelous or other otherwise unlawful, abusive, or obscene material, or constitute the misappropriation of trade secrets of any third party;

III disparage the products or services of any third party; or

IV contain any personal information (other than your email address or user name).

7. Disclaimer of Warranties. CCP disclaims any and all responsibility or liability for the accuracy, content, completeness, legality, reliability, or operability or availability of information or material contained on the Web Site. CCP disclaims any responsibility for the deletion, failure to store, misdelivery, or untimely delivery of any information or material in respect to the Web Site. CCP disclaims any responsibility for any harm resulting from downloading or accessing any

information or material on or thorough the Web site. All materials, including, but not limited to, annual reports to shareholders and press releases reproduced on the Web Site speak as of the original date of publication. The fact that a document is available on the Web Site does not mean that the information contained in such document has not been modified or superseded by events or by a subsequent document or filing. CCP has no duty or policy to update any information or statements contained on the Web Site, and therefore, such information or statements should not be relied upon as being current as of the date you access this site. Moreover, any portion of the materials available on the Web Site may include technical inaccuracies or typographical errors. Changes may be made from time to time without updates to either the Content on the Web Site or the Software and other products provided on the Web Site.

THE PRODUCTS OR SERVICES OFFERED ON THE SITE ARE PROVIDED OR LICENSED 'AS IS' WITH NO WARRANTIES WHATSOVEVER. ALL EXPRESS, IMPLIED, AND STATUTORY WARRANTIES, INCLUDING, WITHOUT LIMITATION, WARRANTIES OF MERCHANTABILITY, FITNESS FOR A PARTICULAR PURPOSE, AND NON-INFRINGEMENT OF PRORIETARY RIGHTS, ARE EXPRESSLY DISCLAIMED TO THE FULLEST EXTENT PERMITTED BY LAW. TO THE FULLEST EXTENT PERMITTED BY LAW, CCP DISCLAIMS ANY WARRANTIES FOR SECURITY, RELIABILITY, TIMELINESS, AND PERFORMANCE OF THE PRODUCTS AND SERVICES OFFERED ON THE WEB SITE. TO THE FULLEST EXTENT PERMITTED BY LAW, CCP DISCLAIMS ANY WARRANTIES FOR OTHER SERVICES OR GOODS RECEIVED THROUGH OR ADVERTISED ON THE WEB SITE OR RECEIVED THROUGH ANY LINKS PROVIDED ON THE WEB SITE, AS WELL AS FOR ANY INFORMATION OR ADVICE RECEIVED THROUGH THE SITE OR THROUGH ANY LINKS PROVIDED ON THE WEB SITE. CCP SIMILARLY DISCLAIMS, TO THE FULLEST EXTENT PERMITTED BY LAW, ANY WARRANTIES FOR ANY INFORMATION OR ADVICE OBTAINED THROUGH THE WEB SITE.

YOU UNDERSTAND AND AGREE THAT ANY MATERIAL DOWNLOADED OR OTHERWISE OBTAINED THROUGHT THE USE OF THE PRODUCTS AND SERVICES OF THE WEB SITE IS AT YOU OWN DISCRETION AND RISK AND THAT

YOU WILL BE SOLELY RESPONSIBLE FOR ANY DAMAGES TO OR CLAIMS IN RESPECT THEREOF, INCLUDING WITHOUT LIMITATION, YOUR COMPUTER SYSTEM OR LOSS OF DATA THAT RESULTS IN THE DOWNLOAD OF SUCH MATERIAL.

Some jurisdictions do not allow the disclaimer of implied warranties. In such jurisdictions, the foregoing disclaimers may not apply to you insofar as they relate to implied warranties.

8. Limitation of Liability. IN NO EVENT WILL CCP, OR ANY OF ITS AFFILIATES OR SUBSIDIARIES, BE LIABLE FORANYDAMAGES,INCLUDINGWITHOUTLIMITATION, DIRECT OR INDIRECT, SPECIAL, INCIDENTAL, OR CONSEQUENTIAL DMAGES, LOSSES OR EXPENSES, INCLUDING, BUT NOT LIMITED TO, LOST PROFITS, DISCLOSURE OF CONFIDENTIAL INFORMATION, LOSS OF PRIVACY AND LOSS OF USE, ARSISING IN CONNECTION WITH THIS SITE OR USE THEREOF OR INABILITY TO USE BY ANY PARTY, OR INCONNECTION WITH ANY FAILURE OF PERFORMANCE, ERROR, OMISSION, INTERRUPTION, DEFECT, DELAY IN OPERATION OR TRANSMISSION, COMPUTER VIRUS OR SYSTEM FAILURE, EVEN IF CCP, HF, OR AFFILIATES THEREOF, ARE ADVISED OF THE POSSIBILITY OF SUCH DAMAGES, LOSSES OR EXPENSES. IN ADDITION, IN NO EVENT WILL CCP, HF BE LIABLE FOR ANY ACT OR OMISSION OF ANY THIRD PARTY INCLUDING, BUT NOT LIMITED TO, ANY PROVIDER OF TELECOMMUNICATIONS SERVICES, INTERNET ACCESS OR COMPUTER EQUIPMENT OR SOFTWARE OR FOR ANY CIRCUMSTANCES BEYOND ITS CONTROL INCLUDING, BUT NOT LIMITED TO, FIRE, FLOOD OR OTHER NATURAL DISASTER, WAR, RIOT, STRIKE, ACT OF CIVIL OR MILITARY AUTHORITY, EQUIPMENT FAILURE, COMPUTER VIRUS, OR FAILURE OR INTERRUPTION OF ELECTRICAL, TELECOMMUNICATIONS OR OTHER UTILITY SERVICES.

Some jurisdictions do not allow the exclusion of certain warranties or the limitation or exclusion of liability for incidental or consequential damages. In such jurisdictions, the foregoing limitations may not apply to you.

9. Indemnification. You agree to indemnify and hold harmless CCP and its affiliates and subsidiaries from and against any claims arising out of or relating to:
   (i) content you submit, post to or transmit through the Web Site;
   (ii) your connection to the Web Site;
   (iii) your violation of this Agreement; or
   (iv) your violation of any rights of any person in connection with the Web Site.
10. Governing Law. THIS AGREEMENT SHALL BE GOVERNED BY AND CONSTRUED IN ACCORDANCE WITH THE LAWS OF THE STATE OF ICELAND, WITHOUT GIVING EFFECT TO THE CONFLICT OF LAW RULES OF SUCH STATE
11. Amendments. The terms of this Agreement may be amended by CCP from time to time. In such event, CCP will post the amended terms on the Web Site. If you use the Web Site after we post such a change on the Web Site, it will constitute your agreement to the revised terms. You may terminate this Agreement by not using the Web Site if you do not agree with any such amendment.
12. Termination. CCP, may suspend or terminate your use of the Web Site at any time, without notice for any reason and accordingly deny your access to the Web Site. CCP has sole discretion in determining whether to terminate your access to the Web Site. You may also terminate your own use of the Web Site by refraining from using the Web Site. Upon the termination of your use of this Web Site, whether termination is by CCP or according to your own discretion, you must promptly remove, delete, or destroy all materials downloaded or otherwise obtained from the Web Site, as well as all copies of such materials, whether made under the terms of the Agreement or otherwise.
13. Assignment. You may not assign the Agreement to any other party. CCP may assign the Agreement to any current or future, directly or indirectly, affiliated company and to any successor of CCP. CCP also may delegate certain rights and responsibilities under the Agreement to independent contractors or other third parties.
14. Miscellaneous. This Agreement constitutes the full agreement between you and us related to the use of this Web Site. If any provision of this Agreement is held invalid or unenforceable, all other provisions

will remain in full force and effect. We may choose not to exercise or to delay enforcement of any of our rights under this Agreement without losing them. Use of the Web Site will constitute your signature to this agreement and evidence that you have read, understand, accept and agree to the terms of the Agreement. You may print a copy of this Agreement for your records.

Copyrights

The Content on the Web Site is protected under Iceland, U.S., and foreign copyright, trademark and other laws. All the Content is the property of CCP, its content suppliers, or its affiliates. You may not modify, publish, transmit, participate in the transfer or sale, create derivative works, or in any way exploit any of the Content, in whole or in part. CCP authorizes you to view and download a single copy of the Content for your personal, non-commercial use. No copyright is claimed as to any material in the public domain, such as United States federal, state or local government information. **CCP hf.**

Grandagarði 8
101 Reykjavik
Iceland

Bibliography

Bauman, Z. (1998). *Globalization: The Human Consequences*. New York: Columbia University Press.

Beier, K. (2008). 'UM-VRL: Virtual Reality – A Short Introduction'. http://www.vrl.umich.edu/intro/

Boellstorff, T. (2010). *Coming of Age in Second Life: An Anthropologist Explores the Virtually Human*. Princeton, NJ: Princeton University Press.

Butler, J. (1999). *Gender Trouble: Feminism and the Subversion of Identity*. London: Routledge.

Caoili, E. (2010). '*Second Life* Creator Restructuring, Laying Off 30 Percent'. Gamasutra. http://www.gamasutra.com/view/news/28892/Second_Life_Creator_Restructuring_Laying_Off_30_Percent.php

Carse, J. P. (1987). *Finite and Infinite Games*. New York: Ballantine Books.

Castronova, E. (2007). *Exodus to the Virtual World: How Online Fun is Changing Reality*. New York: Palgrave Macmillan.

Ching, F. (1979). *Architecture: Form, Space, and Order*. New York: Van Nostrand Reinhold.

Culler, J. (2009). *Literary Theory*. New York: Sterling.

Debord, G. (1967). *Society of the Spectacle*. Reprinted Online: Marxists Internet Archive. http://www.marxists.org/reference/archive/debord/society.htm

Edwards, B. (2007). 'The History of Civilization'. Gamasutra. http://bit.ly/civ-history

Eliade, M. (1959). *The Sacred and the Profane*. San Diego, CA: Harcourt Brace Jovanovich.

Ellis, W. (2007). '*Second Life* Sketches: Shipwrecked and Abandoned'. Reuters. http://secondlife.reuters.com/stories/2007/05/11/second-life-sketches-shipwrecked-and-abandoned/index.html

Evans, W. (2009). *Building Library 3.0: Issues in Creating a Culture of Participation*. Oxford: Chandos Publishing.

Franchi, J. (1995). 'Virtual Reality: An Overview'. ERIC Digest EDO-IR-95-5. http://www.planetfreebook.com/Classic_collection/classic_books_author_F_PDF_edited_filenames/Franchi.Jorge!Virtual%20Reality-An%20Overview.pdf

Heim, M. (1993). *The Metaphysics of Virtual Reality*. Oxford: Oxford University Press.

IMDB (2010). 'Memorable Quotes from *The Office*'. Internet Movie Database. *http://www.imdb.com/title/tt0386676/quotes?qt0444980*

Simcity (2010). 'Inside Scoop' http://simcity.ea.com/about/inside_scoop/sc_retrospective02.php

'Inventor of the Week: John Underkoffler' (2007). *Inventor of the Week Archive*. Cambridge, MA: MIT School of Engineering. http://web.mit.edu/invent/iow/underkoffler.html

Juul, J. (2005). *Half-Real: Video Games Between Real Rules and Fictional Worlds*. Cambridge, MA: MIT Press.

Kafai, Y., Heeter, C., Denner, J. and Sun, J. (2008). *Beyond Barbie and Mortal Kombat*. Cambridge, MA: MIT Press.

Lanier, J. (1989). 'A Vintage Virtual Reality Interview'. Originally published at Whole Earth Review (this version accessed at: http://www.jaronlanier.com/vrint.html).

Landow, G. (1994). *Hyper/Text/Theory*. Baltimore, MD: Johns Hopkins University Press.

Lury, C. (1996). *Consumer Culture*. New Brunswick, NJ: Rutgers University Press.

Mielke, J. (2007). 'Capcom art director Daigo Ikeno discusses Street Fighter IV's visual style'. 1UP.com. http://bit.ly/daigo-ikeno Nicholson, S. (2010). *Everyone Plays at the Library: Creating Great Gaming Experiences for All Ages*. Medford, NJ: Information Today.

Nitsche, M. (2008). *Video Game Spaces: Image, Play, and Structure in 3D Game Worlds*. Cambridge, MA: MIT Press.

Parlett, D. S. (1999). *The Oxford History of Board Games*. Oxford: Oxford University Press.

Rushkoff, D. (2009). *Life, Inc.: How the World Became a Corporation and How to Take it Back*. New York: Random House.

Schulze, J. (2010). 'Making Future Magic'. BERG Blog: http://berglondon.com/blog/2010/09/14/magic-ipad-light-painting/

Sirius, R. and Jude, St. (1996). *How to Mutate and Take Over the World*. New York: Ballantine Books.

Strickland, J. (2007). 'How Virtual Reality Works'. HowStuffWorks.com. http://electronics.howstuffworks.com/gadgets/other-gadgets/virtual-reality.htm – 23 June 2010.

Starkman, N. (2007). 'What Students Want: Leave Me Alone . . . I'm Socializing'. Chatsworth, CA: THE Journal.

Stegner, W. (1969). 'Wilderness Letter', in *The Sound of Mountain Water*. Harmondsworth: Penguin.

Swalwell, M., & Wilson, J. (2008). *The Pleasures of Computer Gaming: Essays on Cultural History, Theory and Aesthetics*. Jefferson, NC: McFarland & Co.

Tiffin, J, and Terashima, N. (2001). *HyperReality: Paradigm for the Third Millennium*. London: Routledge.

Turner, V. (1967). *The Forest of Symbols*. London: Cornell University Press.

'Visuals' (2010). 'Street Fighter IV', http://en.wikipedia.org/wiki/Street_Fighter_IV

Wardrip-Fruin, N., & Harrigan, P. (2004). *First Person: New Media As Story, Performance, and Game*. Cambridge, MA: MIT Press.

Wardrip-Fruin, N., & Harrigan, P. (2007). *Second Person: Role-Playing and Story in Games and Playable Media*. Cambridge, MA: MIT Press.

Wark, M. K. (2007). *Gamer Theory*. Cambridge, MA: Harvard University Press.

Weber, A., Rufer-Bach, K. and Platel, R. (2008). *Creating Your World: The Official Guide to Advanced Content Creation for Second Life*. Indianapolis, IN: Wiley.

Wolf, M. (2002). 'Genre and the Video Game', *The Medium of the Video Game*. University of Texas. Chapter 6 Rpt. in: http://www.robinlionheart.com/gamedev/genres.xhtml

Index

FSC
www.fsc.org
MIX
Papier | Fördert
gute Waldnutzung
FSC® C083411

Kolibri 360 GmbH
Ferdinand-Jühlke-Straße 7
99095 Erfurt, Deutschland
produktsicherheit@kolibri360.de